S0-BNB-230

the Making of a Pastoral Person

the Making of a Pastoral Person

Rev. Gerald R. Niklas

ALBA · HOUSE NEW · YORK

SOCIETY OF ST. PAUL, 2187 VICTORY BLVD., STATEN ISLAND, NEW YORK 10314

Library of Congress Cataloging in Publication Data

Niklas, Gerald R
  The making of a pastoral person.

  Includes bibliographical references.
  1. Pastoral theology—Catholic Church. 2. Lay
ministry—Catholic Church. 3. Catholic Church—
Clergy. I. Title.
BX1913.N57   253   80-26978
ISBN 0-8189-0409-7

Nihil Obstat:
John J. Jennings
Censor Librorum

Imprimatur:
†Daniel E. Pilarczyk, Vicar General
Archdiocese of Cincinnati
March 12, 1980

The Nihil Obstat and Imprimatur are
a declaration that a book or pamphlet is considered
to be free from doctrinal or moral error. It it is not implied
that those who have granted the Nihil Obstat and
Imprimatur agree with the contents,
opinions or statements expressed.

Designed, printed and bound in the United States of
America by the Fathers and Brothers of the
Society of St. Paul, 2187 Victory Boulevard,
Staten Island, New York 10314, as part of their
communications apostolate.

FORDHAM
UNIVERSITY
LIBRARY
NEW YORK, NY
LINCOLN
CENTER

1 2 3 4 5 6 7 8 9 (Current Printing: first digit).

© Copyright 1981 by the Society of St. Paul

DEDICATION

Dedicated to my family whose love and concern I value highly and to Joe, Dick and Steve who have significantly influenced my life

PREFACE

Since the Second Vatican Council has stated that ministry is an obligation of all baptized persons, a question has been raised concerning the characteristics a person needs to possess to minister effectively. Those involved in setting up programs for training lay persons in ministry ask what qualities their prospective applicants should have. Those engaged in formation work of sisters, brothers and priests question themselves in the same way—what are the necessary ingredients for effective ministry to take place?

Knowing who we are as ministers (having a clear pastoral identity) and being comfortable with our own feelings and others are clearly essential to effective ministry from my experience as a chaplain and as a supervisor in Clinical Pastoral Education. However, there are many aspects to this quality of being comfortable with feelings.

Authority is one of them. In this day of collegiality how much authority should pastoral persons claim? If pastoral persons view ministry as valuable, it is certainly appropriate for them to claim some authority. How much authority is acceptable, if at the same time pastoral persons are trying to imitate the humble carpenter who washed the feet of his apostles. Anger is present in ministry; pastoral persons can't please everybody all the time. It's important for ministers to be able to deal with their anger as well as that of others. Sometimes, people are angry at them for what they did or didn't do. Other times they are angry at God, the Church or their pastor and choose to ventilate to any minister whom they happen to meet. Should pastoral persons try to defend themselves, God, the Church or their pastor? Ministry to angry persons is becoming more and more important today.

Sexuality arises in ministry, just as it does in all facets of life. Pastoral persons can't hide behind their Roman collar or garb, pretending it doesn't exist. It does and needs to be dealt with if effective pastoral care is to be given.

Group dynamics constantly face pastoral persons who are members of many committees and participating in innumerable meetings. Ministers benefit from knowing how to facilitate meetings when they are chairpersons and what to do when a passionate plea for a return to the basic facts of religion is followed by silence. Is the chairperson to presume that one member is speaking for all the others? How is the chairperson to break the silence and to get the meeting started again? Many of us attend a number of worthless meetings. We need to know how to enable others to face that fact. A knowledge of Erik Erikson's eight stages are helpful to ministry too. How can pastoral persons minister to an elderly person who enjoys recalling stories from his younger days? Why do some hospitalized persons seem to go through such trauma in taking some tests while others have no problem with them. Erikson's stages can easily be applied to sick persons and assist in understanding them.

Spirituality, one of the most important qualities for a minister to have, gives depth and richness to a person's pastoral identity. It enables pastoral persons to sink their roots in the Lord so that they avoid the temptation to become social workers instead of ministers. It also has a tremendous integrating force with the other qualitites which pastoral persons possess.

This book is intended to be a stimulus to those engaged in ministry, those preparing for ministry and to all persons seeking to respond to their baptismal call. It is the result of eight years of struggling to become more fully human myself and of supervising students in pastoral care in hospital settings which have programs accredited by the United States Catholic Conference or the Association of Clinical Pastoral Education. Some of these pages are the result of my own experiences as a human being in search for more wholeness which has occurred from receiving counseling. Some are the result of my personal and professional growth as a basic student in Clinical Pastoral Education. Some I have gleaned as a supervisor-trainee under the direction of Rev. Richard A. Donnenwirth while others have come as a result of learning from over 100 students whom I have supervised. All these have helped me in my journey and I believe by sharing them others will be assisted in their ministries.

I am deeply indebted to Katherine Boehmer and Noreen Henkel who have typed and retyped these chapters innumerable times. A great debt of gratitude is also due to Anne Gander and Kathy Miltz who have read the manuscripts with a critical eye and offered many helpful suggestions in improving this work. Finally, I thank the editor of *Sisters Today* for granting permission to print chapter three which appeared in that magazine before revision for insertion in this book. The quotations from the Bible have been taken from *The New American Bible*.

TABLE OF CONTENTS

the Making of a Pastoral Person

CHAPTER ONE

PROCESS OF PASTORAL EDUCATION

In my own training for the priesthood, I entered the seminary in September and for the most part never left it except for a two week vacation at Christmas, a one week vacation at Easter and a three month vacation in the summer. I never experienced any kind of co-op program where there was an attempt to integrate lofty theological principles and ideals with the "nitty gritty" of life. My preparation to meet the needs of people took place in isolation from people and their real problems. In contrast to that kind of training, I believe educating persons for any kind of ministry in the Church today needs to be based on relationships, experiences, reflection and evaluation, emotionality, integration and decision-making. As persons live in the world and interact with it, they relate to people, experience people and events, reflect and evaluate some of these experiences, emote because of these interactions, integrate some of them into their personalities and make decisions in everyday living. Pastoral care education is a process, based on this understanding of life and assumes that these are necessary for true education. This process is assisted in supervised pastoral care programs such as those present in general hospitals, mental health centers, jails and other centers certified by the National Association of Catholic Chaplains and/or the Association of Clinical Pastoral Education.

Relationships

Supervisors relate to students as leaders and this leadership is exercised in a manner in which there is a high degree of sharing responsibility and deciding together. Yet, it is assumed that education doesn't take place totally by concensus, but is assisted by some structure, e.g. weekly schedule. Supervisors relate to students as co-workers, as persons with whom they are working together, rather than as persons who are working for them. Supervisors don't give their students all the "leg work" or unload their duties on the students, but relate to them more as colleagues than superiors, as coaches more than lecturers. In this function as coaches, the leaders scrimmage with the supervisors at times in the daily work of pastoral ministry and, at other times, simply stand on the sidelines and watch, waiting for a time-out to offer suggestions.[1] Functioning in this capacity, the supervisors are tempted to engage in "disciple hunting," that is, to have the students model themselves in many aspects of pastoral care. Aware that this is one of the "special difficulties" involved in the supervisory process, they periodically examine their relationship to the students.[2] Aware that there is bound to be some modelling of supervisors, they periodically bring this to the students' attention. At the same time, they raise the issue of the modelling the students' parishioners do of them in their parish setting. Finally, they relate to the students as pastors conveying their concern for them as individuals and as students in process. Sometimes this is manifested by supporting them to give them the strength they need to continue their ministry. Other times it takes the form of confrontation, challenging them to use their full potential.

Because of these kinds of relationships between supervisees and supervisors, supervision differs from the classroom setting where teachers are usually viewed as persons who have all the answers or where teachers pour all the right techniques into the students. It's also different from the classroom because the supervisees are pastors in the fullest sense of the word because they are fully responsible for those persons to whom they minister in the C.P.E. Center.[3]

In addition to the relationship between students and supervisors, there are many other relationships in this educational context. Ekstein and Wallerstein use the clinical rhombus to illustrate some of these relationships. To convey their idea it is sufficient to modify their clinical rhombus as follows:

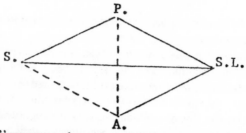

The "S" represents the student, the "S.L." the supervisor or leader, the "A" the administrator, and the "P" the patient or parishioner. Thus, there are several lines of communication, not just one. This rhombus could be expanded to include the staff, the patients' families, and the student's peers, because all of them are interacting with the student as she/he engages in a pastoral care education program. Such an enlarged rhombus would point out the complexities of interaction and communication and, consequently, the potentials of parallel process and problems in learning.[4] They also suggest potentials for transference and counter-transference. The full value of the rhombus is grasped when it is contrasted with the vertical line method of interacting as follows:

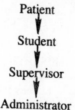

Experiences

From interacting with all these various people, students gain many experiences. In a hospital setting, as they relate to nurses and other people who are caring for the sick in different capacities, they perceive people who are functioning in a very professional manner and who are confident and competent in their work. Some students are so overawed by this professionalism that their anxiety increases. Another result of interacting with these other professionals is that often it causes the students to reflect on their unique contribution to the patient's welfare as clergy persons. In addition, as the weeks go on, the supervisees see the human side of their professional peers and perceive them as imperfect, as not always giving the best care. This, in a sense, gives them permission to be less than perfect in their ministry.

In ministering in this kind of setting, students experience some patients and their families who are joyous because the patients are preparing to be dismissed after successful surgery and experience others who are very upset because the doctor has just informed them of a terminal illness. As a result, the students have the opportunity of rejoicing with one family and comforting the other in their sorrow. They encounter the "good patient" who never reveals any of his feelings and is eager to meet the expectations of the staff, as well as the "difficult patient" who is never pleased by anything the staff does. They minister to patients who have little or no knowledge of God, those who claim not to believe in God and others who have an intense relationship with their Creator. They experience people who have the same value system as they do and others who believe in God but have a radically different value system.

Reflection and Evaluation

In order for these experiences to be profitable, the students need to reflect and evaluate them. Writing verbatims is an excellent means to assist this process because in so doing the students analyze their own response to determine their degree of effectiveness. The students check themselves to see where they switched the subject on the patient and reflect on their reason for doing so; they reflect on the appropriateness of gathering as many medical facts as possible from the patient; they evaluate "why questions" to see if they put people on the defensive; they determine the effectiveness of "closed questions" as opposed to "open-ended questions." Further, they evaluate their introduction to the patients when they enter their room to determine if it is conducive to effective ministry and their manner of leaving the room at the conclusion of a visit. One student, for example, introduced himself in such a manner that it seemed like he was apologizing for visiting patients. So he was asked to reflect on the value of his visit to the patient's welfare and challenged to reflect on his pastoral identity.

The students are assisted in the process of reflection and evaluation by their supervisor and peers. With this assistance the students are not only challenged to determine the reason some responses are ineffective, but also to reflect why others are effective. In addition, alternate methods of responding to patients and their families are indicated so that it becomes clear that there are a number of effective ways of ministering. Sometimes the patients, their families, and the staff enter into this process by giving the students feedback on their ministry.[5]

Emotionality

As students reflect and evaluate their ministry, they are given the opportunity to consider how their feelings or emotionality assist or block their ministry. Initially many students are unaware of the influence feelings have on ministry and presume that ministry to the sick occurs simply through a head-to-head exchange with a patient or through prayer and reading the Bible. They miss the opportunity to interact on a person to person level. One student who was struggling with her own fear of cancer attempted to minister to a cancer patient who began sharing depressed feelings about his illness. The student became uncomfortable and tried to reduce her uncomfortableness by switching the subject to positive aspects of his life and urged the patient to "be thankful because you have such a wonderful wife to help you with your sickness." So it is important for the students to be challenged to come into contact with their feelings about various kinds of illnesses so that they can be more effective in their ministry to the sick. It's especially helpful to realize their feelings about pain, bodily deformity, becoming dependent on others for performing the daily chores of routine living, becoming aged, being forced into retirement, and dying.

In addition, the students are urged to come to grips with feelings in general in the interpersonal group, in their supervisory session and in their many other interactions with people in the educational process. For most students this is difficult because of the low value our culture places on feelings. This difficulty is enhanced by many religious cultures which emphasize the tremendous value of the intellect over the emotions and by the frequent restrictions religions have placed on the expression of "negative" feelings, e.g., anger or hatred.

When students realize how their feelings influence their ministry, they arrive at the "teachable moment." Jerome Brunner, in writing about the process of education, says that the task of teaching a subject to a child at any particular age is one of representing the structure of that subject in terms familiar to the child's way of viewing things. Transferring this to supervision, it means that when the "teachable moment" comes, the student learns because supervisors or peers present the material in a manner congruent with the student's way of experiencing life.

Integration

In the educational process, students learn many techniques and theories about pastoral ministry in their classes and in the books recommended for their reading, but they are only beneficial if students integrate them into their personal and professional identities. Unless this occurs, these techniques and theories are merely extensions of the students who appear cold and wooden, using them in their ministry. Another effect of a lack of integration is that the convictions the students express have no depth. Patients quickly sense that the supervisees are simply speaking to them from the "head," rather than sharing "gut feelings." One student who had great difficulty in expressing anger, urged a patient to ventilate her anger because it would be helpful to her total well-being. Because of the student's own difficulties in sharing her anger, the patient did not perceive the expression having any sincere conviction behind it. Generally, it takes months and years before some of these principles truly become part of a person and integrated into the total human being.

Further, students are challenged to integrate the total educational experience with their theological principles so that the program is truly Clinical *Pastoral* Education. If this theological integration fails to occur, then there is little or no difference between a counseling program and a clinical pastoral program, and as a result the students' theology and clinical work are compartmentalized rather than blended together. Students are enabled to integrate their theology with clinical experience by participating in morning devotions, by having a section of theologizing in each verbatim, and by having classes in theological reflection in which they analyze case studies in bioethics, e.g., determining to allow this baby to die or to perform many costly operations to enable it to live, examining the principles behind a student's decision to baptize this baby and not to baptize another, reconciling a loving merciful God with tragedy.

Decision-Making

Finally, decision-making is an aspect of education, and the students' decision to embark on the educational pilgrimage is a significant one. Sometimes students seek acceptance in a program because some authority person (e.g., director of the lay pastoral ministry program) demands it and so reluctantly they commit themselves to the program. If students maintain that attitude during the program, their lack of total committment naturally affects their participation. They begrudgingly do their assignments, and display their hostility by turning in their assignments late and not presenting any matter for the supervisory conferences. Before students begin, it's beneficial to urge the students to reexamine their decision "to sign up" for the program to offer them a second chance to make the decision their own instead of someone else's.

Another significant decision for the students is to decide how much authority to claim for themselves and how much to give to their supervisor. Some students are so deferential, they claim no authority and constantly seek advice from the supervisor how to do this and that. Others adopt the attitude "nobody is going to tell me what to do" and so they are constantly rebelling. It is beneficial for the students to examine their normal pattern of responding to authority to determine if they would like to change it. The students form a contract as the program begins in which they commit themselves to the general expectations of the program and discuss with the supervisor some particular aspect they find objectionable to see if some agreeable adjustment can be made.

The students continue to make decisions as the program proceeds. They need to decide whether they are going to take risks to grow or not. One student was fearful of stepping into the unknown and so remained closed in spite of attempts to enable him to share himself. Another student came with a burning zeal to develop her potential to the fullest and so tried new ways of relating to the patients and her peers, new methods of responding to feedback, and a new manner of interacting with authority. The students chose to relate deeply with people or only superficially; chose to have as many experiences as possible or just a few, etc. As the program comes to a close, the students decide how they plan on using the knowledge and skills they have acquired. Some students, thrilled with their growth, plan to utilize their new skills in their ministry and intend to continue some kind of pastoral education in their own communities.

Others decide one quarter of pastoral education is sufficient for their ministerial growth and aren't interested in any other programs.

It is essential that the students realize they have the power to make decisions in all aspects of their lives. No one forces them to become angry and to throw things; no one forces them to marry or to choose celibacy; no one forces them to enter the field of pastoral care. These are options in life which they choose and they are responsible for their choices. Sometimes they are tempted to excuse themselves, blaming their parents or the spirit of our day for their actions. However, this is not valid. God gave all of us intellects and wills and so we freely choose, to do this and not that; we make decisions every day of our lives and need to take responsibility for them.

Finally, it is important for the students to realize they are responsible only for their own decisions and can't take responsibility for other's decisions. They aren't responsible because one of their patients chooses to remain depressed and makes no effort to adjust to the partial paralysis of his right side as a result of a stroke. Nor can students take full responsibility for the effect their decisions have on others. One student might choose to eat lunch with the nurses from his unit while his peers resent this because they want all the students to share lunch together. This student is not responsible for the resentment his peers feel toward him. Although he might have some responsibility to share the reason for his decision with them. Thus, students benefit from realizing they have only partial control over life and not complete control.

Conclusion

This educational theory presumes the existence of relationships, experiences, reflection and evaluation, emotionality, integration and decision-making. It presumes that because all these elements are present, the goal of education is attained—helping students grow by stimulating them to test and develop their assumptions. In this process, the students are assisted in becoming independent and possibly later to become friends and permanent co-workers of their supervisor.[6] Further, this educational theory assists in achieving the goals of pastoral care education programs: to better equip the students for ministry by inviting them to get in touch with themselves, by improving interpersonal relationships, by enabling students to make their theology more relevant and by developing professional skills in pastoral care to sick persons, the staff and their parishioners.

Footnotes

1. Oates, Wayne E., *Pastoral Psychology*, "Pastoral Supervision Today," Fall, 1975, p. 24.
2. Schuster, Sandt & Thaler, *Clinical Supervision of the Psychiatric Resident*, Brunner/ Mazel, Inc., (New York, 1972).
3. Oates, Wayne E., *Pastoral Psychology*, "Pastoral Supervision Today," Fall, 1975, p. 28.
4. Ekstein and Wallerstein, *The Teaching and Learning of Psychotherapy*, (Basic Books, 1958). p. 138.
5. Nash and Mittlefehdt, *Amer. J. Orthopsychiatry*, "Supervision and the Emerging Professional," January, 1975, p. 94.
6. Ekstein and Wallerstein, *The Teaching and Learning of Psychotherapy*, (Basic Books, 1958), p. 80.

CHAPTER TWO

TOOLS USED IN SUPERVISION OF
PASTORAL EDUCATION

The goal of pastoral education is to have the students test their assumptions and to develop their own theories concerning effective ministry. This does not take place overnight, but rather occurs over a period of time with the assistance of a supervisor and some structure. The students need supervision, a process which enables them to evaluate their ministerial functions and pastoral identities. This is done with the supervisor, using his/her educational theory (the material presented in the previous chapter) as guidelines for the supervision. In Clinical Pastoral Education, the structure includes verbatim sessions, interpersonal groups, supervisory conferences, didactic sessions, a daily journal, midterm and final evaluations, and experiences of the students pastoring patients and staff. They are assisted in this process not only by their supervisor, but also by their peers, the other professional staff, the patients and their families.[1]

Screening Interview

Supervision begins with the screening interview which offers an opportunity to determine if the prospective candidate meets the criteria for admission, namely, sufficient educational background, emotional stability, pastoral identity, sufficient motivation and a willingness to be supervised. It is not necessary that the candidate be enrolled in the seminary, but that the person have some religious formation in a formal setting like that given to a deaconess, a religious woman in a convent or a participant in a lay pastoral ministry program.

For the sake of the patients and the other participants in the program, it is important that the applicant is emotionally stable. Sometimes religious superiors who lack an understanding of the purpose of Clinical Pastoral Education (C.P.E.) refer their disturbed personnel, thinking it will be a substitute for therapy. Although there are some similarities between therapy and supervision, they are very different. If the major portion of time is spent with the students' inner problems, that is therapy. If the major portion of the time is spent discussing the patient's problems, even though some time is spent with the students' problems that are interfering with pastoral care, then it is supervision. If a student has some personal problems, possibly she/he could engage in therapy and at the same time be supervised in pastoral care in C.P.E.

A pastoral identity which separates the pastoral person from a social worker and a secular counselor is also important. One applicant, for example, said she did not believe in God and as a consequence never prayed. Such a person is well-intentioned, but is not suited to function as a chaplain. During the interview the applicant is informed of the goals of the programs and the necessity of participating in the classes, verbatims, etc. and the supervisor attempts to determine if the prospective candidate has sufficient motivation to meet these and other demands of the program. Sometimes students apply for a program simply because they are told to do so, rather than because of personal motivation. Finally, the applicant needs to give evidence she/he is "superviseable," that is, open to change and growth, and is not intending to use the program only as a means to gain conversions to a particular denomination.

To assess whether the prospective candidates meet the admission criteria, they are asked to describe their strengths and weaknesses or to give five adjectives that describe them and five others that do not. The prospective candidates are asked to describe their mother or father to determine whom they model and to describe their present significant relationships and their support system. It is important too for them to relate some major event in their life and the meaning they attach to that. Finally, they are requested to relate how they handled conflict and anger recently in their lives. From the responses to questions like these, the supervisor knows if the persons can benefit from a C.P.E. program, something about their emotionality, and some of the supervisory issues that will occur.

Supervisory Conference

Another part of the supervisory process is the supervisory conference where the supervisor checks his/her emotional responses with the supervisee who does the same with the supervisor. In the didactic sessions, it's a head-to-head interchange for the most part, while in the supervisory conference the emotions come into play. Both share their feelings and monitor them, trying to determine their cause. If a supervisor becomes sleepy during a supervisory session, she/he tries to determine the reason, e.g., because the supervisee is resisting, taking a "head trip," or because she/he never got enough sleep. In doing this, the supervisor makes a distinction between "old feelings" that she/he brings into the conference and "new feelings" sparked by the interaction with the supervisee. In one supervisory session, Joe began offering excuses for not having his verbatims in on time. He has done this before, blaming it on a broken typewriter, stalled car, etc. The supervisor was tired of this and shared his irritation with him. As a result, Joe stopped his excuses and simply said he was sorry he didn't have it. The next time when he began making excuses, the supervisor simply interrupted him and asked him to monitor what he was doing.

During the supervisory process, the supervisor gains many insights into the students and is tempted to share them. However, this is only done if the supervisor intends to deal with these issues in detail. One student, Elizabeth, repressed her sexual feelings, but the supervisor chose not to deal with them and instead chose to deal with the goals she wrote for herself.

An issue that often surfaces in supervision and generally in all aspects of the program is that of authority. The supervisees struggle to assume their own authority and, deciding how much authority they will give to the supervisor. Another aspect of the authority issue is for the supervisor to determine how much authority the supervisor demands and how much she/he encourages the students to own for themselves. The supervisor is aware of these authority issues and lifts them up for the students in a manner and at a time that will facilitate their growth.

Learning Contract

Another tool of supervision is the learning contract which the students form in the first days of the program. An important part of the contract are the goals the students set for themselves. In a supervisory session these goals are discussed to determine if they are realistic, specific, and related to the goals of C.P.E. Sometimes students want to change them as a result of this discussion and other times the supervisor asks for a change. However, it's best to allow the students to keep their goals if possible because they are more motivated to attain them if they are their own. At midpoint in the program, the supervisor and the students examine the goals together to see if any changes are appropriate.

Parallel Process

The students are assisted to achieve their goals when they allow the patients to become their teachers. This takes place when there is awareness of the parallel in the dynamics existing in the relationship between the supervisor and the supervisee and that existing between the supervisee and the patient. This is called the parallel process and it has two uses. First, as the supervisees relate to their supervisor, they relate to the patients. Joe usually avoided every question the supervisor asked him about his feelings as his verbatims were being examined. As Joe constantly avoided feelings in his relationships with patients. Whenever the patients were on the verge of sharing their "negative" feelings about illness, he urged them to think positive. So as Joe related to his supervisor about feelings, he also related to patients—a general avoidance of them.

A second use of parallel process indicates that as the supervisor relates to the students, they in turn relate to their patients. Since students are relating to an authority figure in this instance, they might be more active or passive than usual. However, the parallel still exists and is a good teaching tool. A supervisor frequently confronted Mike about his avoidance of anger in ministering to the patients and with his tardiness in coming to class and in handing in verbatims. In relating to a 27 year old female patient who has been very angry with her mother for 13 years, Mike confronted her concerning her continued anger and asked her why was she unwilling to give it up. As the supervisor used confrontation in dealing with Mike, so he utilized it in ministering to patients.

Affirmation and Confrontation—Means to Growth

To facilitate growth in the students, the supervisor uses a mixture of affirmation and confrontation. In my own growth as a person, I profited from both and think that other students do too. The supervisor affirms the students' unique strengths and reinforces what the students do that is effective in ministry. Having received this support, the supervisees are given the strength to lower their defenses and try new methods and new styles of behavior.[2]

From the New Testament we know that Christ is the perfect representative of the affirming person because he loved each person precisely as she/he was, yet at times we know he confronted people with their shortcomings. Christ affirmed Simon Peter when he professed his faith in him as the Messiah, the Son of the Living God, but later confronted Peter because of his denial, asking three times, "Peter, do you love me?" Christ mixed affirmation and confrontation in his interaction with the Samaritan woman at the well. He affirmed her by his acceptance of her which was indicated by his countenance and by gently engaging her in conversation, "Give me a drink." After she said, "I have no husband," Jesus confronted her in his reply, "You are right in saying you have no husband. The fact is, you have had five, and the man you are living with now is not your husband." (Jn 4:18). Thus Jesus accepted her as she was and at the same time invited her to become a better person.

Resistance

Sometime during the program, the supervisor usually meets resistance to personal and professional growth from the supervisees. This resistance[3] which is conscious and unconscious is manifested when the students change the topic, relate a lengthy story or fail to hand in their assignments. By these tactics they express a desire more to maintain the status quo than to risk the insecurity of change. On the one hand, the students want to learn, but at the same time are afraid to risk themselves. Even though trust has been established between the supervisor and the supervisees, this is not enough to overcome their resistance. Some information or suggested change is too threatening for the students to accept because it attacks their self-image and so it is blocked out or interpreted in such a way as to pose less of a threat. All of us have perceptual screens which filter out or distort communication that makes us feel uncomfortable. Adults especially, have self-images that are more resistant to accept knowledge from others which demands a change.

To reduce the resistance the supervisor not only affirms the students' current strengths, but also identifies with them to bridge the gap between him/herself and the students. To do this, the supervisor and students seek out together where agreement exists among them and then the supervisor helps them become aware of the feeling that appears to be behind the resistance. Often, it is fear directly or indirectly. The supervisor assists the students further by focusing on the work context, instead of on their differences. For example, Frank announced to the group he wasn't going to present any more verbatims because the group criticized him too much. To reduce his resistance, the supervisor recalled his contract in the first days of the program where he agreed to participate in verbatims, and also mentioned how awkward it would be for him to comment on his peers' verbatims and not to present any for them to comment on.

Students are assisted immensely in ovecoming resistance if they become aware of resistance in one of their patients. Frank was helped when he encuntered a patient who resisted his efforts to discuss cancer and his feelings about it. The harder he pushed her to talk about the life threatening disease, the more she resisted. The supervisor pointed out the parallel to him between his patient's resistance and his own when Jean kept urging him to stop withdrawing from the group. The more she demanded he return, the more he avoided her.

Searching For Options

Supervision enables the supervisee to seek and evaluate other options. When the supervisor functions in this way, there is no need to proselytize, nor to seek an extension of him/herself in the students. Rather this approach enables the pastoral person to become a professional, to achieve self-realization. Such a supervisor is not tempted to over-identify with the students because this kind of leader identifies with the process of supervision itself.[4]

An effective use of searching for options occured with Jean. She came one week late for the program and during the first supervisory session asked how could she make up the time. Instead of giving her the answer, the supervisor asked her how she thought this could be done. She said she could stay a week after the program was over, but she didn't want to do this. Then two other options were presented, working after supper or on weekends. She chose some evenings and two Saturdays from the various options.

Pastoral Identity

The development of a pastoral identity is a crucial issue usually for pastoral persons because their pastoral effectiveness is severely hampered by personal identity that is not integrated with a professional identity. If a supervisee's personal identity is arrested at a certain stage in his personality development, e.g. adolescence and he is perceived as an adult capable of providing ministry, then his incongruity expresses itself in anxiety. This anxiety is only a symptom of the real problem, the lack of an integrated pastoral identity.[5]

Role confusion also seems to stem from a lack of a clear pastoral identity. A supervisee who has not struggled to attain his own pastoral identity easily adopts some of the roles of the other professionals with whom he works. In analyzing 150 verbatims over a two-year period, I discovered that a number of the students in a C.P.E. program in a hospital adopted the roles of (a) the medical person by asking and giving medical information, (b) the social worker by obtaining information about social security and nursing homes for the patient, (c) the ''joy-boy'' by having a strong need to cheer up all the patients, (d) the problem-solver by listening to the patient's problem for a while and then offering a solution, and (e) the ''super-professional'' by hiding behind his/her profession with so much stiffness that the patient has no feel of the person as a human being.

Freud explains that the development of the personal identity lies in the context of the family, basing it on the tender love of the parents for the child. Erikson develops his concept more fully and offers implications for the development of a professional identity.[6] Briefly, as the students grasp an understanding of their own emotional history, they comprehend their own continuity better which enables them to establish their personal identity. Their pastoral identity grows out of this personal identity, as well as out of an identification with some significant pastoral person e.g. their supervisor or their pastor and by engaging in pastoral responsibilities.

It is important to make a clear distinction between a program designed for psychiatric residents or students in social work and students in pastoral care. Sometimes students from all these programs are dealing with the same issues with a patient. Sometimes they are even using the same psychological tools, but the whole orientation is different with students in a C.P.E. program. Clergy persons have a pastoral identity while the others have medical or social identities. In order to communicate to the students the theological orientation of the program, morning devotions are helpful. More helpful are weekly theologizing sessions in which the participants are challenged to re-think their theological beliefs and to investigate whether they have a solid basis for a certain theological practice or opinion. So this process influences them to re-read their theology so that they sharpen their thinking on various theological issues, and more importantly, it helps them to integrate their theology with their daily living. What value is theology if it is isolated from their day-to-day living? Finally, this process challenges the participants to explain their theology to their supervisor and peers in clear terms.

Supervisor as a Learner

The supervisor learns from using the parallel process. She/he also learns by evaluating the effectiveness of her supervisory style with the supervisees during the program and as the program concludes. It is beneficial to offer the supervisees an opportunity to participate in such an evaluation. Finally, it is important for the supervisor to continue learning by pastoring patients in the setting where the supervision occurs. In doing this, the supervisor meets some of the personnel the students work with, continues to increase ministerial skills, and grows in understanding the students better, since she/he periodically will experience some of the same anxieties that the students do. So the supervisor is an educator, a pastor, and a learner. In order to facilitate this learning, the supervisor has available consultation because others (who are less close to the situation) often offer profitable insights.

In conclusion, an effective supervisor is an eternal learner, and as such helps the supervisees by identifying with their activity and process of constant growth, rather than with static opinions that have become frozen dogmas of limited usefulness. Supervising and learning are then mutually interdependent to maintain genuine professional identity.[7]

Footnotes

1. Nash and Mittlefehdt, *Amer. J. Orthopsychiatry*, "Supervision and the Emerging Professional," Jan. 1975, p. 98.
2. Conrad W. Baars, *Born Only Once*, (Franciscan Herald Press, 1975).
3. Robert Langs, *The Supervisory Experience*, (New York: Jason Aronson, Inc., 1979), pp. 85, 326, 444.
4. Ekstein and Wallerstein, *The Teaching and Learning of Psychotherapy* (Basic Books, 1958,) p. 80.
5. Max R. Maguire, "Hang-Ups in Chaplain-Patient Relationship," *Addresses and Workshop Papers*, "College of Chaplains," New Orleans, La., January 13-14, 1969.
6. Erik H. Erikson, *Childhood and Society*, (New York: W.W. Norton, 1950).
7. Ekstein and Wallerstein, *The Teaching and Learning of Psychotherapy* (Basic Books, 1958), p. 80.

CHAPTER THREE

IDENTITY AND COMFORTABLENESS
WITH FEELINGS

"Here it is only three o'clock and I'm finished! I visited the first half of the unit yesterday and saw the other 20 patients this afternoon." A statement like this is typical from a student beginning training in hospital visitation because he is usualy anxious about his visits and as a result generally makes very superficial, brief encounters. This same student told me six weeks later, "You shouldn't assign so many patients to the next group. I simply can't visit them adequately."

As his supervisor, I rejoiced in his growth because that comment and his verbatims (written records of his pastoral conversations with patients) indicated he was ministering on a deepening level with his patients. Consequently his visits took longer and were more beneficial. He had moved in his conversations from the "weather" and a superficial "how are you" to some real concerns because now he was relaxed, and as a result so were the patients. When he first began ministering at the hospital, the patients noticed his nervousness and so kept the visits short, for his sake as well as their own.

I have examined over 150 verbatims of some twenty students I supervised in Pastoral Care Education programs and have notice many common characteristics among them. I would like to share these with you and then draw a couple of conclusions.

Initial Anxiety Evident by Frequent Use of Questions

Since most of the students had little acquaintance with hospitals it was normal for them to be anxious about their initial visits with sick persons.

As the quotation at the beginning indicates, some pastoral care students handled their anxiety by visiting many patients very briefly. Others coped with their anxiety by asking a number of factual questions so that there were no pauses in the conversation. One asked five factual questions as he began his conversation with the patient, and then relaxed enough to allow for a brief period of silence and for the patient to take the lead in the conversation. Another student who began the program with some skill in counseling, was able to relax more quickly and allowed the patient to introduce the topic of conversation, indicating by his responses he was listening. He interacted with the 70 year old patient who had been hospitalized more than a month for major surgery, in the following manner:

C-1:　　Hello, Mrs. X. Are you doing any better today?

P-1:　　Well, I'm all right. . . . I guess. You know I've been out of bed and have been up and walking around.

C-2:　　Yes, I saw you in the hall yesterday and you seemed to be doing pretty well.

P-2:　　I guess I'LL HAVE TO BE discharged soon.

C-3:　　I'm sorry. . . . I don't think I follow. You say you'll HAVE TO BE discharged?

P-3:　　Well, if I'm discharged soon and I can't go back to my appartment . . . you know what that means?

C-4:　　No, not exactly, but go on, Mrs. X.

This interaction clearly keeps the focus on the concerns of the patient.

Forming A Pastoral Identity

Another problem that arises for many students deals with their pastoral identity. Seminarians are not alone in experiencing this difficulty; religious women and priests encounter similar problems, especially those entering the pastoral field from teaching or nursing. Some of us have never taken a good look at exactly who we are as persons. When people ask us who we are, the immediate response is seminarian, sister, priest. A priest never relates to a nun, a nun never relates to a postman, and a housewife never relates to a teacher, but rather we relate to people who happen to be religious women, priests, housewives and teachers. We don't relate to roles, rather to persons who have individual roles. Unless our own identity is clear as persons, we tend to be quickly aware of our insecurity when we encounter other people. In our uncertainty about our personal identity, we find it difficult to affirm other people in their personhood. So the real questions are, Who are we personally? What are we feeling? What do we value highly? What do we disvalue? What relationships are important to us, if any? What are our natural strengths? What skills do we have? What are our weaknesses? It is important for all of us in pastoral care to know our emotions, relationships, strengths, weaknesses, values and goals. Then we realize our personal identity; we know ourselves as persons.

Our personal identity is attained by receiving feedback from other people. If we are open to being affirmed by others, we understand our own goodness, we understand that we have certain gifts and can do certain things well. This means we are open to receiving compliments from other people. At the same time, our own identity is attained by rejecting the expectations that other people place on us. This is especially necessary for religious who receive many expectations from others because of their role. If we accept the expectations of others, then we adopt the "ideal self" and never discover the "real self." In addition to being open to having our goodness affirmed by other people, it's also necessary to accept the painful realization we can't do everything. We have certain limitations and that is acceptable. We are still good persons.

Lay persons entering the field of pastoral care have to struggle with these same issues as well as viewing themselves as "chaplains" or "ministers." One student could not bring herself to introduce herself as chaplain to the patients because she was so steeped in the concept from her early Catholic training that only the priest is the chaplain. Because lay ministers are not ordained, they too struggle with their identity as "ministers."

Since our pastoral identity flows from our personal identity, we develop our own pastoral identity once we know who we are as persons. An authentic pastoral identity does not emerge from a fuzzy or fake personal identity. We must know who we are individually before we are ready to determine the role we want to exercise in the ministry to the sick; we are prepared to determine how our functions differ from those of a nurse, doctor, social worker or a friendly visitor.

Another important factor in determining our pastoral identity is our model of Church. If our model is "institutional" with an emphasis on hierarchical authority, we will function differently than if our model is "servant" with an emphasis on love and service. Our pastoral identity will differ from both of these if our model of Church is "community" which sees the Church not as a visibly organized society nor as a group of persons seeking to be of loving service to others, but as a communion of persons united primarily by interior bonds of creed and ecclesiastical fellowship. Thus each model of the Church influences our pastoral identity and each has its strengths and weaknesses. It is profitable for us to realize, as we form our pastoral identity, that model or those models of the Church upon which we rely heavily.[2]

Confusion of Pastoral Identity

Because some students entered the program without having any insight into their pastoral identity, they immediately adopted the role of *the medical person*. They asked many medical questions of the nursing staff and attempted to acquire a quick course in medicine. In visiting patients, occasionally this role or confusion was so great that there was no difference between their visits and that of a medical resident. Unfortunately, it even happened that pastoral students delighted in their new knowledge and displayed it in the presence of the patient. One informed the patient why his surgery had to be postponed instead of allowing a medical person to impart this information. The pastoral student said:

"When they ran the test, they found a slight fluctuation in your heart—something like an irregular rhythm in your heart beat. When your family doctor told them that you had had this for a long time and that it would not affect the operation, they decided that it would be okay."

Other pastoral students perceived their pastoral identity as "*problem-solvers.*" They listened very carefully to discover the patient's problem and then offered a solution. Undoubtedly, many of them modelled themselves after their own pastors whom they saw function in this manner. Possibly, they were treated in this manner by their pastor when they were struggling with some difficulty, and so they adopted the same model of behavior. One patient who was hospitalized for rehabilitation therapy to gain the use of her legs was troubled when her 60 year old husband suddenly began wearing very sporty clothes, bought a bicycle exerciser and did not seem to want her to come home unless she could walk by herself. The student not only gave advice, but possibly raised new anxieties for his patient in his fifth response to her:

"It seems to me that your husband might be afraid of getting old. Both of you getting ill at the same time after many years of health and doing things together has been interrupted. I think he is afraid of being disabled. He has recovered from his condition and is trying to keep it that way. But a wheelchair at home is a reminder of what might happen to him."

Some of the students saw themselves as "*cheerleaders,*" visiting patients to cheer them up. Nursing personnel often regard the chaplain in this light, saying, "Mr. X. seems lonely today. You might try to cheer him up." At other times, the nurses express this idea in giving pastoral persons information concerning patients on the unit with special needs. "No, everybody seems pretty good today. Nobody is down." So, this role is placed on the clergy and it's easy for them to accept it wholeheartedly if they don't have a strong pastoral identity. A side benefit from accepting this role is that the pastoral person thereby gains the acceptance of the nursing staff. One student used this approach so much that initially he seemed like a salesman. On closer examination though, it seemed that this was his way of gaining acceptance from his patients and a method he employed to keep the patients from discussing feelings, especially those of fear and anger.

In struggling to establish an identity, other students saw themselves as *"persons of prayer"* to the extent that they felt compelled to pray with every patient, whether the patient wanted a prayer or not. It appeared that pastoral persons thought they had failed to fulfill their duty unless they prayed with each patient. Briefly, these students had a far greater need for prayer than did the patients. One student stated her goal in the first minute of the interview:

> "I've come to see you and to promise you my prayers, both this evening and tomorrow morning. If you wish, I'll pray a little surgery prayer with you now."

For some students, this essential element of their identity was *"professionalism."* Some stressed this so much they were incapable of expressing any warmth and seemed as though they were hiding behind their profession. One student constantly used the phrases "we think" and "we believe" and so I kept wondering in reading his verbatims what he personally thought about any given topic. This same student spoke to patients as though he were quoting from some textbook. His whole bearing was so professional that he was artificial and there was no opportunity for the patient to see the real human person who was a pastoral person.

What a contrast these styles were to that of another student who was sure of his pastoral identity and walked with the patient in his pain. This student interviewed a 20 year old university student, hospitalized for minor surgery and this is how the conversation flowed:

C-1:   How's it going, Joe?
P-1:   Pretty good, I'm pretty sure I'll be leaving tomorrow.
C-2:   I guess you're kind of happy about that.
P-2:   Yes I am. I'm kind of anxious to get back to work.
C-3:   So that you don't fall behind?

P-3:   Right . . . (a pause for a few moments) . . . You know I'd still like to talk to you about why I'm not practicing my religion.
C-4:   Go ahead, Joe.
P-4:   Well, it is not that I think religion isn't important, but I see people at Mass who are nothing more than hypocrites.
C-5:   Hypocrites?
P-5:   Yeah . . . they act like they're really holy.
C-6:   And this phoniness you see really bothers you.

This student's clear pastoral identity enabled him to listen to the patient's concern, to encourage the patient to share it completely and to give the patient the feeling of being understood and accepted.

Discomfort With Feelings

One of the most common problems that students experienced was discomfort with the world of feelings. Since many seemed to be totally unacquainted with feelings, they frequently became very uncomfortable when patients tried to talk about how they were really feeling. In addition to having a clear pastoral identity, comfortableness with feelings is the most important aspect of pastoral care.[3] Sometimes seminary faculties and religious superiors argue that feelings are not important and teach almost total reliance on the intellect. Students with this attitude were of limited help to patients initially because they could not enter their world of fear, pain, depression, anger, etc. One of the easiest ways of avoiding the feelings of the patient was simply to act as if they were not there. A student, who was very adept at sidestepping feelings generally followed a patient's expression of feelings with a factual question or statement. A 50 year old widow who had to retire early because of a heart condition verbalized her struggle to adjust to the retirement and he immediately responded, ''Do you have any hobbies to occupy your time?'' Another response which would have conveyed to the widow she was understood might be: "I guess this early retirement is really difficult for you to adjust to."

Other students used a little different approach to achieve the same goal. One student asked 13 questions in 15 responses and another 8 in 10 to stay in control of the conversation in order to stir away from any discussion of feelings. Another student pressed his own agenda in speaking with patients and also used prayers to attain his goal—discussing facts only. These students reminded me of an old TV detective program "Dragnet" in which Jack Webb played the part of the chief detective. He always appeared on the screen soon after some woman discovered a dead body and naturally was very upset. Jack Webb's famous response to this woman in distress was, "Just the facts, ma'am, just the facts." These students had their own indirect way of expressing the same wish—"just the facts, please no feelings."

After being in the program a few weeks, some students rapidly learned to become comfortable with mild, positive feelings. They were relaxed in comforting patients and families who were crying, were comfortable with small silences and were able to rejoice with those patients who were recovering successfully from surgery. However, it took quite some time before the students learned to deal effectively with *anger or depression and other feelings which are often viewed as "negative."* This is not surprising since our Christian training gave us the idea that these feelings were bad or not fitting for us Christians who have the assurance that the Good Shepherd will never leave us wanting. The old examination of conscience booklets come to mind where we are questioned under the fifth commandment whether we ever became angry.

One patient whose doctor deprived her of cigarettes expressed intense anger toward her doctor to the pastoral student who replied: "You know, I'm wondering if your condition is more serious than you want to admit to yourself. Those cigarettes must be very bad for you." Clearly this response did not give the patient the feeling of being understood and accepted, but instead was an attempt to move the patient to the factual aspect of her condition.

Other milder feelings of this kind like *fear and worry* were avoided too by the students who displayed their anxiety not only by controlling the topics of conversation but also by attempting to control people—manipulating them into feeling how the clergy wanted them to feel. This tendency was especially common among those students who were former teachers. This is not surprising because for years they had been in a classroom struggling to keep control over the children and trying to mold them into good Christians. No doubt, at times they used manipulation to achieve this goal. In ministering to patients, some of them easily fell back into their old habit.

Attempting to manipulate patients' feelings to keep everything "nice" seems to be another trait for some former teachers. To keep things "nice," one former teacher told a 46 year old man on the eve of his surgery, "When the report turns out good tomorrow, you'll be sorry you worried about the surgery." Another former teacher who was experiencing difficulty adjusting to the fact that she was no longer teaching to teenagers told a 69 year old widow, suffering intense pain over the past four years, "It's just silly to worry about taking medication to reduce the pain." This admonition was given, even though the patient expressed fear about the adverse side effects drugs have on people. In addition to manipulating the feelings of patients, some former teachers had a tendency to "talk down" to patients as these examples indicate.

Discomfort With Discussing Death

In spite of all the programs today on death and grief, there were still many students who were uncomfortable with these topics. They reacted to them like some of the other topics of a feeling nature—just act like nothing significant had been said. Other students imitated some of the nurses and doctors in reacting to dying patients—they simply avoided visiting them or spent a very brief time with them. One pastoral person showed his uneasiness with a dying patient by standing some distance from him and avoiding touching him when that would have been appropriate. Others concealed their uneasiness as this student who in his verbatim simply avoided the topic when a 70 year old patient opened the door to discuss it.

Patient: I don't watch my diet as I should. But at my age I think I should be able to be a little careless if I want to. I have had a good life and am ready to go whenever the time comes.
(pause)

Pastoral Person: Are you feeling better today?

Other students were not only afraid of discussing death, but also any *disease that might lead to that topic*. One student had the technique of changing the subject when a patient spoke of cancer. On one occasion a woman mentioned to him in the hallway that she had just been informed that her husband had cancer. He carefully avoided the issue saying, "You are Mrs. X, aren't you? I met you the other day when I was visiting your husband. I am sorry that I did not recognize you away from your husband." If patients are going to be ministered to effectively, we in pastoral care need to invite them to discuss any topic.

Discomfort With Intimacy

Another characteristic I noted in the students was their discomfort with intimacy. Some have not revealed much of their personal lives to anyone and so were anxious when a patient began pouring out his innermost secrets to them. They simply didn't know how to handle this kind of sharing. Some attempted to ease their nervousness by changing the subject as one student did when his patient mentioned she was living in sin since she was married outside her Church. Other times they simply expressed their shock to the patient as happened when a woman confessed that her husband, a confirmed alcoholic, went to a bar sometimes and just stayed there until he was completely drunk. The student responded: "Is his problem that bad?" A more pastoral response might have been, "No doubt, this has been difficult for you."

Conclusion

I have generally mentioned instances from verbatims of students where their lack of a clear pastoral identity, of an awareness of their own feelings and of an ability to minister to the feelings of patients has hindered their pastoral effectiveness. However, there were many other occasions where they interacted effectively with the sick. For example, after a 53 year old lady told a student she had suffered much in her life, he felt comfortable enough to walk with her in her pain by asking her a very open question, "How has your suffering affected you?" After some weeks in the program, another student felt comfortable with silence and viewed it as a profitable time for the patient to think and come in touch with his feelings. Because of this, he simply remained silent as he nonverbally displayed his concern for a 66 year old man who said, "I received some bad news today, but it's hard to put it into words."

Sometimes, too, students were appropriately assertive with patients by not allowing them to drift from one topic to another and by urging them to share their feelings. The evening before surgery, one patient mentioned he was upset about the operation, but failed to say more about it. The woman chaplain responded, "Would you like to talk more about what upsets you concerning tomorrow's surgery?" This invitation indicated she was comfortable to be emotionally available to the patient.

Fr. Henry Nouwen, in an article in *America*, "Compassion: Solidarity, Consolation and Comfort,"[4] urged pastoral care persons to be compassionate in our ministry by manifesting our human solidarity as we cry out with those who suffer, to console patients by feeling deeply the wounds of life and to offer comfort by pointing beyond the human pains to glimpses of strength and hope. He went on to say that the greatest compliment we can receive from a patient is, "That person really understands me and, as a result, I feel comforted."

Footnotes

1. Bernard J. Busch, "Intimacy and the Celibate Life," (tape) Kansas City, Mo., *National Catholic Reporter*, 1978.
2. Avery Dulles, *Models of the Church*, (New York: Doubleday and Co., 1978).
3. Philomena Augudo, "Religious Women as Pastoral Ministers" *Emmanuel*, Dec. 1978, pp. 593-4.
4. Henry Nouwen, "Compassion: Solidarity, Consolation and Comfort," *America Magazine*, March 13, 1976, pp. 195-200.

CHAPTER FOUR

FEELINGS

In ministering to another, we relate to the whole person with our whole person. We don't relate simply as professionals. Rather in ministry, our whole being becomes involved, and this includes our feelings and the feelings of the people to whom we are ministering. We relate to the other members of the healing team too and this means we relate with our feelings as well as theirs. (I wish to credit John L. Wallen, Ph.D. for the seminal thoughts present in this chapter.)

Dealing with these feelings of ours and those of other people is the greatest source of our difficulty in our interpersonal relationships in ministry. This is a very broad statement, but it can be supported, if we reflect on some recent incident in our own lives. How often when someone began describing how bad things are going for them, did we hear the phrase, ''Cheer up, don't let it get you down,'' or ''It's silly to feel that way.'' Pastoral persons who are having difficulty dealing with their feelings after ministering to a family after a tragic death might say, ''I don't know why I feel this way but . . . ,'' or possibly in an argument it is said, ''Let's keep emotions out of this and look at it more rationally, let's try to be more objective.'' It seems that we spend a lot of time and energy trying in one way or another to ignore or deny our own feelings, or the feelings of others. Actually, we are having feelings every day of our lives, but we tend to view them as upsetting. In effect we are saying it's a problem being human because we are experiencing human feelings.

Another reflection supporting our difficulties with feelings is to examine how often we share feelings directly with the person about whom we are experiencing them. We mention to our friend that we are very angry because our boss reprimanded us, or that we feel loving and grateful toward our boss because he went out of his way to do us a favor. But notice that we are not telling that particular person our angry or loving feelings, but verbalizing them to someone else. Another aspect of this issue is the time perspective. When did those feelings occur? Often we find few discussions of feelings which a person is presently experiencing in comparison with the number of discussions about past feelings. A person might say, "One month ago when you told me you weren't going on vacation with me this year, that really hurt me." This person is relating a feeling, but it is a feeling that is three weeks old. If we look at the way we human beings interact with one another, we will discover that we ignore feelings by talking to someone else about the feelings we have toward a particular individual or by talking about past feelings. Dealing with feelings, mine and other people's, is the greatest source of difficulty in interpersonal relationships in ministry.

Humans tend to identify feelings with intentions. If some action of another person makes us angry, we attribute ill intentions toward him and on the contrary, if an action of another person pleases us we attribute loving intentions to him. When someone allows a door to slam in our face, we tend to attribute thoughtlessness to him or think he's angry at us for some reason. In reality though, the person might have something on his mind and be totally unaware we are behind him, yet our tendency is to attribute ill-will toward that individual. On the other hand, there is the tendency to attribute good intentions when another person's action makes us feel good. Recently I went to buy a pair of shoes and while I was trying on the shoes the salesman began telling me how shoes were made and the six possible measurements for a shoe, not just the measurements in the length and width. My initial feelings were very warm toward this salesman for taking the time to explain those interesting facts about shoes because I felt he was being extra kind to give me that useful information. However, ten minutes later he told me quite frankly, he gave me all this information while the new shoes were on my feet so that he could convince me of the shoe's comfort and quality. Then I realized he was kind to me simply to make a sale and so I ceased attributing kind intentions to him.

A second characteristic of feelings is that they serve "a fuse function." Feelings tell us what an individual situation means to us. Feelings tell us whether we are comfortable or uncomfortable, loving or hateful, fearful or relaxed. If we look at an electrical switch box in our homes and find a fuse burned out, the fuse tells us there's something wrong in the circuit. We check it out to see where the overload is, correct that error, and then we replace the fuse. The fuse tells us we have overloaded the circuit before the whole house burns down. Feelings serve a similar function in our interpersonal relations, in the sense that before the relationship is destroyed completely, we feel resentful; before a situation is at the breaking point we feel angry. These feelings are signals indicating that in order to sustain a relationship, we have to check out and examine what is occurring presently between us and another person.

A third characteristic of feelings is that we can focus on them or focus elsewhere. Our power of attention enables us to some extent to select one feeling to concentrate on and to reject another one. If someone urges us to focus on the pressure our watch is exerting on our left wrist, we are aware of it; but before anything was said it was in the margin of our attention. The focus of our attention can change, if someone says, "Be aware of the fingers on your right hand." These fingers were here all the time, but we weren't thinking of them before. Our attention has shifted from the watch on our wrist to the fingers on our right hand. No doubt, a person can refuse to be aware of the sensation on his wrist or the fingers of his right hand, but he can only refuse to focus on these parts of his body, if he intentionally focuses on someone or something besides that. This is what happens when we ignore our feelings, we repress them.[1] Over the years we formed the habit of diverting our attention from feelings to something else. If the cast on our broken leg is itching and we turn the TV on to watch the superbowl football game, then we soon forget our uncomfortableness because all during the game our attention is focused on our favorite team. As long as we are absorbed in the game, we are unaware of the itching; yet the cast is on the leg all the time.

We can do the same thing when we make judgments about other people, instead of being aware of our real feelings, focusing our attention on someone else instead of on ourselves. If our supervisor treats us unfairly, we may feel inadequate and resentful. But instead of focusing on us and our unpleasantness, we focus on the supervisor, saying he is unfair and stupid. By speaking about him in that way, we are trying to take away our uncomfortable feelings. We deny our feelings because they are expressed as his characteristics. By making judgments about another, we keep our feelings in the margin of our attention. Whether feelings are in the focus or in the margin of our attention, they still influence our behavior.

Finally, feelings cannot be controlled by leaving them outside of the focus of our attention. We can only control feelings by leaving them in the focus of our attention and using them to help us diagnose what's going on in the situation right now. For example, a priest called an hour before dinner and asked if he could come to eat with us at the hospital. I said that it was OK, even though I was irritated because I told him on a couple of occasions that the cook needs two hours notice to conveniently prepare for another person for supper. My priest friend came for supper, and after we finished eating, he commented, "This really upset you that I gave you such short notice, didn't it?" I was surprised by that question and asked him how he gained that insight. He replied that initially during the meal I talked constantly with the other hospital chaplain and did not draw him into the conversation at all. I displayed my irritated feelings non-verbally, and did not control them by putting them out of the focus of my attention.

Sometimes there is great emphasis on control and being in control of ourselves as an indication of our maturity. We tolerate a child having a temper tantrum because he's only five, but we look down upon a man who has a temper tantrum. However, it's foolish to think that feelings can be controlled by ignoring or denying them. When we do this, we give up control and allow them to control us. If we feel angry and convince ourselves we don't feel angry, this simply means we've trained ourselves to ignore a set of feelings, to repress them. We can repress our feelings of anger or sexuality, but they still affect our behavior. The method to control our feelings is to be aware of them, to experience them consciously. Then we can control the behavior flowing from the feelings.

Five Basic Emotions

This concept of awareness of feelings is understood more clearly by examining the physiological aspect of the five basic contact emotions. When we are *angry*, our body sends us a clear message communicating our anger. We want to fight physically or possibly verbally; our whole system tells us so because we breathe faster, our heart beats faster, our muscles begin to contract and we actually have a sensation of heat. When we are *fearful* almost the opposite bodily reaction to anger takes place. Our mouth becomes dry, we feel cold, our palms begin to sweat and we have a desire to run away. If we shake hands with someone who is frightened, the cold sweat is quickly evident. When we feel *hurt*, we withdraw and regress as if we wanted to go back into our mother's womb. A common symptom of hurt which we all recognize is crying. However, many of us find it very difficult to display our hurt because in the minds of many people that means we are weak. Women usually feel more freedom to express their pain through tears than men. Another fundamental feeling is *trust*. When we are open with someone, we are saying, "I am comfortable in your presence to the extent that I'm willing to be vulnerable." The opposite of course is mistrust, a feeling of not being free, not being able to be ourselves with one another. When we are not trusting, we hold back and our friends never know what we are feeling or thinking.

The final basic emotion is *love* and again our bodies tell us physiologically whether we are feeling lovable. When we are loving, there is a warm glow about us which we can easily compare to anger which is a hot emotion. So the two feelings are similar. In order to express love we have to take the risk of first expressing the other four feelings, and obviously we can never have a true lasting relationship with another until we are able to fight with that person. When we are able to display our anger toward another, our fear, our hurt and our trust—then we can love. When we can level with each other, telling each other how we feel and allowing our feelings to be shared openly, then we can experience closeness. Thus, love is a fulfillment of all of these other feelings.[3]

If we are struggling to get in touch with these basic emotions we can take comfort in the fact that Carl Rogers admits he has difficulty with some of them. He says he was brought up in a situation where anger was simply not a feeling to be exhibited or expressed. As a consequence when it did come out, it was pretty violent. He acknowledges that over the years, he has become more and more aware of the times when he is angry but that sometimes, he is not aware of it at the moment it is occurring. Another emotion that Carl Rogers admits he has difficulty talking about and has struggled with for a long time was a feeling of warmth and love from others. He admits it is difficult for him to feel good about himself and to understand how others could praise him so highly for something he did.[4]

Levels of Communication

It is valuable for us to be aware of the different levels of communication between people.[5] The first represents the lowest level of communication. At this stage there is no communication unless it happens by accident. People interact very superficially and exchange cliches with one another such as, "How are you? How is your family? How is your job?" Generally people are not really interested in the answers to these questions and are astounded if you ever take such a question seriously and begin answering in detail. Usually the person senses the superficiality and the conventionality of our concern and obliges us by simply giving the standard answer, "O.K." This is the kind of conversation that takes place at cocktail parties, at reunions and meetings. There is no real sharing of persons, and everyone remains at a safe distance from one another.

On the second level there is reporting the facts about others. In this level there is no sharing of anything about ourselves but rather we talk about others, remaning content to tell others what common friends have said or done. There is no personal commentary on these facts, but simply a reporting of them. On this level there is a seeking for shelter in gossip items and little narrations about others. There is no giving of anything of ourselves and no invitation for others to give in return.

In the third level some communication of the person occurs. We are willing to risk telling something of our ideas and revealing some of our judgments and decisions. As we communicate our ideas though, we are watching carefully to test the trust level of the other person. We want to be sure the other person will accept our ideas, judgments and decisions. If the other person raises their eyebrows or narrows their eyes, if the person looks at his watch, we usually retreat to safer grounds. We begin saying things we suspect the other person wants us to say and try to be what he wants us to be.

In the next level the participants have the courage to share their feelings, gut level sharing takes place. Here we go beyond revealing our ideas, decisions and judgments and differentiate ourselves from others by communicating our own feelings about these matters in our lives. In this level we really want others to know who we are and so we share from our gut as well as our head. Many people share ideas and judgments, but the feelings that underlie them are uniquely ours. No one is committed to a political party or to a cause with our exact feelings of fervor or apathy. No one experiences our passions, senses our frustrations, or labors under our apprehensions. On this level we wish to share with others these feelings if we are to reveal who we really are.

When our own reactions are completely shared by a friend, when our happiness or grief is perfectly mirrored in him, we have attained the highest level of communication. We are like two musical instruments playing exactly the same piece of music and giving forth the same sound. In this peak communication which exists among close friends or between partners in marriage, there exists from time to time a complete emotional and personal union, in which one of the persons opens himself in such a way that the other person is called out of himself and out of his old and fixed positions into a new beautiful experience. In our human existence this can never be a permanent experience, but there are moments when an encounter attains perfect communication.[6]

Methods of Sharing Feelings

We communicate our feelings non-verbally in a *physiological manner*, when we realize we made a mistake we feel embarrassed and our face becomes somewhat flushed. This is a physiological non-verbal communication of our feelings. Another manner of non-verbally communicating feelings is *"acting out."* Frequently nurses use this phrase on psychiatric wards describing a patient as acting out her anger by throwing dishes on the floor in the cafeteria. In our lives we "act out" our love for another person by hugging them or our anger by clenching our fist at them.

There are also many ways of *verbally communicating* feelings. The most effective method is to *report feelings* which is done in three different ways. First, we use the word feel followed by a particular kind of feeling or a label. For example, I feel happy, hopeful, sad, mad, glad, angry, hurt, etc. Sometimes we vary this form by simply stating a feeling word and not using the word "feel"—I am happy, hopeful, sad, etc. Another method of reporting feelings is to allow the phrase, "I feel like" with a simile. For example, I feel like a little boy who has been spanked, or I feel like a king, meaning that someone has treated me with special kindness.

A final way of reporting feelings is to follow the phrase, "I feel like" with some particular action. I feel like hugging you—indicating my affection, or I feel like running away from you—sharing my fear. All of these three methods of expressing feelings report what is actually occurring within us and give people clear messages about us.

There are *direct expressions* which also communicate feelings, but their messages are not as clear. These occur when a person gives a command and hidden underneath that expression is a feeling. A teacher in a classroom shouts, "Shut up" and beneath that expression the students know there is anger. One may shout at his friend, "Go fly a kite." Underlying that command, the friend feels his anger. Another method of expressing feelings is done indirectly through a judgment. Instead of being aware of our feelings, we focus our attention on our boss or a friend who has offended us. We say that Tim is stupid or insensitive and beneath those expressions are feelings of hurt or possibly inadequacy. Perhaps the most frequent indirect expresssion is made by a frightened passenger in an automobile when the driver is speeding. Instead of saying, "I'm scared" which is clear reporting of feelings, the passenger beats around the bush with his vague communication, "Do you think it's safe to drive this fast?"

When we report our feelings directly it's helpful to do so in such a manner that our friend doesn't feel coerced to change. Our message is not, "I'm scared, and you slow down," but rather it is "I'd simply like to inform you that I'm scared." A person who is sincerely interested in us will consider that.

Frequently we human beings report feelings vaguely and know the struggle that exists in my own life in being straight forward. This happens because we are not only uncomfortable with feelings in general, but because *we have feelings about our own feelings*. If as a child we threw a book at our brother in an angry argument, our parents probably scolded us for doing this. Unfortunately the message probably picked up is that throwing books and anger are both bad. So we develop a feeling about anger, guilt. If a girl was openly affectionate with her relatives at a family gathering and then criticized for it, she probably learned not only that it is bad to express feelings of affection, but also learned to be anxious about feeling affectionate. As an adult, she does not allow feelings of affection to come into the focus of her attention, but prefers to keep them in the margin of her awareness. She has a feeling about her feelings of affection, anxiety.

Another factor concerning our difficulty in sharing feelings is that at times *we have ambivalent feelings toward others*. We feel very grateful and loving toward our friend, but at the same time feel irritated when he comes half an hour late for a dinner engagement. Possessing loving and irritating feelings at the same time tends to confuse us, until we realize it's possible for us to have conflicting feelings at the same time.

Value of Sharing Feelings

Even though it's valuable to report our feelings clearly, still we may have difficulty in doing this because of previous training. Generally Christian religions urged caution in regard to feelings and emphasized the value of the intellect as a faculty that would lead us more safely to God. This was particularly true in religious communities and seminaries where close friendships were forbidden or strongly discouraged. These were viewed as possibly leading to forbidden sexual activity or at least as being disruptive of community life. Because of this kind of training sometimes we relate to others only through our roles. Possibly because of our anxiety to protect ourselves and our failure to risk, we hide behind our Roman collar or our religious identity and don't relate as persons, abstracting from our own roles and functions. We relate to others only in a professional manner and allow them to know nothing of what is behind that professionalism. Today, though, there is a more positive view toward intimate friendships where there is a deep level of sharing. Many spiritual writers view intimate friendships as a stepping stone leading to a deep union with Almighty God.[7] It is important for religious persons to be able to develop these kinds of relationships, and an essential element to that goal is an ability to share one's feelings. Intimacy demands communication on an intellectual as well as an emotional level and the most difficult feelings to relate are those of hostility, anger and love.[8]

To appreciate the value of sharing our feelings we might reconsider the first sin of mankind. God gave Adam a command to share and reveal himself to Eve and gave Eve a similar command to share and reveal herself to Adam. However, instead of revealing and sharing themselves, they decided to be mysterious, to hide from each other, to put on masks and to deceive one another concerning who they really were. Instead of openness and sharing entering into the world, deceit, mystery and sin came upon man. This resulted in isolation of man from man and ultimately isolation of man from his God. Obviously, one of the primary benefits resulting from sharing on a deep level is a close relationship with another person. There is a real meeting of the other person where he/she lives. Another benefit is that we have the warm feeling of being understood and of being supported. There is an equal opportunity for us to understand and support the other person, which produces an enjoyable feeling. A third benefit is to discover some patterns of immaturity on our part, to gain insight concerning some aspect of our personalities that we might want to change. Because this is said openly, we not only know it, but have the courage to risk changing. If we consistently seek out friends for the sake of support, sooner or later the question arises why we need so much support. We may come to the realization that we don't accept the compliments people give us and value ourselves more highly. Another benefit of this type of communication is that it tends to create honesty and openness in others. Because we are open and honest, other people tend to follow our example. Because we are willing to risk sharing our feelings, another person feels free to trust us to share his.[9]

Deep communication makes our ministry effective because it enables us to deal with our feelings before we attempt to minister to others' feelings. When we enter into a patient's room, it is important we leave our baggage outside the patient's room. This means that we deal with our feelings of fear of cancer, of dying and of tubes before we enter that room. If we are very fearful and try to repress our fears as we are interacting with the patient, our energy is being used in repressing our fears and consequently not in being present to the patient.[10] There are also occasions when it is important to deal with our feelings while we are interacting with the patient. Sometimes while we are visiting a patient, feelings suddenly rise within us. One method of dealing with those feelings is to share them with the patient. "Your cancer frightens me too, and just as you don't know how to respond to it, I don't know how to respond to you as you tell me that today the doctor gave you the bad news that you do have cancer."

Sharing Gut Level Communications

While I have advocated and wholeheartedly endorsed the value of gut level communications, I think there needs to be certain guidelines concerning its use.[11] The first guideline is that gut level communications never imply a judgment of the other. It is simply unreal to expect we can judge the intention or motivation of another. We need to be realistic enough to admit the mysteriousness and the individuality of another human being and thereby realize we cannot know that person's motivation. We don't have X-ray eyes and the only way we can know another person's intention is to ask him. When we are emotionally honest with another person, there is no judgment present. If we say, "I am uncomfortable with you," we are being emotionally honest and are not implying in the least that it is his fault that we are ill at ease. We are not saying it is anyone's fault, but only reporting our feelings toward this particular situation at this time. Perhaps it is our own "hang-up" of authority or our own uncomfortableness with our sexuality that causes us to be uncomfortable. Let's take another example. "I feel hurt by what you said." Again we are not implying any judgment. Perhaps, we have difficulty dealing with differences and this makes us feel hurt. Or perhaps, we have feelings of inferiority and so need a great deal of support. When we don't receive that support, we feel rejected and hurt.

The second guideline is that emotions are good. All feelings are good. They are not indifferent and certainly not bad in themselves. God created our feelings to help us live a rich, full life. Moral values cannot be placed on sexual urgings, anger, trust etc. However, they can be placed on the actions that flow from these particular feelings. We have been taught that certain feelings are good and others are bad; some are acceptable and others are unacceptable. The truth is that feelings are simply a part of being a human person and sin can only enter the picture depending on what we decide to do with the feelings we are experiencing.[12]

Today in some encounter groups there is a heavy emphasis on getting in touch with one's feelings and in sharing all feelings with everyone. While I encourage sharing, at the same time I do not encourage total sharing with everyone because this is spiritual exhibitionism and can be harmful. When this philosophy of total sharing of all feelings is put into practice by two depressed people, the results can be disastrous. One person says, "Everything is going wrong and I'm depressed;" and another person responds, "I'm depressed too. Let's commit suicide together." One person adds to the other person's depression by his inappropriate sharing. There is equal emphasis in some groups on "acting out" one's feelings and no emphasis on responsibility for those actions. The message here is "if it feels good, do it." Certainly I discourage this kind of behavior just as strongly as I discourage repressing feelings. However, in the third guideline, I encourage integrating our feelings with our intellect and will. Such an integration indicates our maturity, while our immaturity is manifested by allowing our feelings to control our life. It's one thing to admit we feel sexually aroused by a particular person and an entirely different matter to attempt sexual activity with that individual.[13]

In the interplay between feelings, intellect and will it is important to realize that our intellect helps us to be aware of the feelings we are experiencing and that this is an asset to us. The intellect, in turn, presents these feelings to the will in order that appropriate decisions are made. There is a beautiful interaction between feelings, intellect and will and we do not place more value on the intellect than on feelings nor do we place more value on feelings than on the intellect or the will. All three are very important for functioning effectively as a human being.

The fourth guideline is that gut feelings are usually reported. If we wish to share ourselves with another, then we reveal our feelings whether we intend to act upon them or not. We share our anger with our friend without implying in any way that he is the cause or that we intend to hit him. We share our feelings of love without implying that we intend to engage in sexual activity with that person. If we are to open ourselves to another, we allow that person to experience us as we are; we share with him/her our hurts, our fears and our love. Recently a doctor who was a hospital patient beautifully illustrated this before his operation for removal of a cancerous tumor. On the eve of his surgery he broke down and cried in the presence of his friends and simply said, "I'm scared." Thereby, he shared himself with others.

Psychosomatic medicine indicates that many illnesses are caused by repressed emotions that find an outlet through headaches, skin rashes, allergies, asthma, common colds, aching backs or limbs, and high blood pressure etc. This means we are unable to bury emotions. They remain in our subconscious minds and intestines to harm us. It is not only conducive to deep friendship to share our true feelings, but it is equally beneficial to good health.

The most common reason offered for not wishing to share our feelings with our friends is that we don't wish to hurt them. However, we hurt our friends by not sharing ourselves with them openly, and by our coldness or indecision. Another fear we have in sharing our feelings with others is that we suppose people will reject us because some emotions might be viewed as unacceptable. As mentioned earlier, we have feelings about some of our feelings. We are ashamed of some of them and rationalize we cannot report them because they would be misunderstood or disturb a peaceful relationship. These reasons are not valid because any relationship that is built on anything less than openness and honesty is built on sand.

The fifth guideline is that with rare exceptions emotions are reported at the time they are being experienced. It is much easier to report a feeling we had two weeks ago or two years ago rather than to admit right now we are very angry with a friend. When we have the courage and honesty to share our feelings at the time they are occurring, then our relationship can achieve a high degree of intimacy, and indicates there is a high level of trust between us.

Emotions are like a good glass of wine which we savor and drink very slowly. We become deeply aware of the feelings that we are experiencing and know them in the depths of our being. Then we decide how we are going to share them and when we are going to share them. Occasionally, it is inappropriate to share the feelings here and now because a person cannot accept that. If a person has just received word that their parent is seriously ill, it would be inappropriate to share our anger at that time because of something he did a few moments ago before he received that news. Our intellect and will come into play in deciding how we share our emotions. If we become extremely angry with a friend, our emotional urge might be to hit him, but our will guides us to express our anger in a manner to facilitate our relationship rather than destroy it.

Not only between friends are there rare occasions when we would defer the sharing of our feelings, but there are exceptions to this rule to defer or eliminate the reporting of our feelings in the case of a passing incident with a person we hardly know. The irritation we feel at the discourtesy of another driver on the highway might be better kept to ourselves. In the case of two persons who work or live together, or want to relate deeply with one another, this emotional reporting at the time that the feelings are experienced is important.

Conclusion

Many of us are quick to respond to any situation with intellectual responses, and never look inward to see what are our real reactions and feelings. I am reminded of a husband and wife in a married couples' group where the moment the husband finished talking, the wife was right there with her statement which did not allude to his at all. She was constantly waiting for a pause in order to give him her response. A group member stopped her short and said, "Did you hear what he said?" She responded, "Of course I did." However, when she was asked to recall what he said, she thought and thought but embarrassingly could not give any hint of his statement. Then she turned to her husband and finally said, "What did you say?" In other words, she not only did not listen to his ideas, but she never listened to the feelings below those ideas because her own feelings at those times were, "I'll win the argument over you, I'll get in my two cents worth that will be much better than what you have just said." She was totally unaware of this. In order to minister effectively to other pastoral care persons and people in our various settings, we have to listen, not only to their ideas but to their feelings.

Many people are unaware of their feelings at the time they are occurring, but they may become aware of them much later. It takes practice and self training to think, "What is my reaction at this moment? Am I frightened? Am I anxious? Am I angry? Am I feeling affectionate? What is it I am feeling right now?" Sometimes we know we are feeling something, but don't know exactly what it is. We have to give ourselves a moment or two to find out. Initially, getting in touch with our feelings is done quite consciously and then gradually it becomes automatic. It becomes automatic to look inward to recognize what we are feeling and then to be willing to express it in almost all interpersonal relationships. Aware of our feelings, we can use them very constructively in our interpersonal relationships with our fellow ministers and with the people to whom we are attempting to minister.

By being in touch with our feelings, we can also be in touch with certain beliefs that underlie these feelings. As a priest, for example, I may believe I should be respected. When courtesy is not shown to me, I feel angry and hurt. Being aware of these feelings I can challenge my belief to see whether I want to change it. Or, we may feel that we need a particular person's friendship, and that we can't get along without it. This is an irrational belief. It is true we need friendship, but we don't absolutely need the friendship of any one individual. We can receive support from several sources and not just one. If we believe we need friendship from one individual only, then we become depressed if that individual dies, or if the person refuses friendship. This is an irrational belief that must be challenged. Behind our feelings are beliefs, and it's profitable for us to be aware of the beliefs or assumptions we have accumulated over the years in order to be more effective pastoral persons.[14]

Footnotes

1. Thomas A. Kane, *The Healing Touch of Affirmation*, (Whitinsville, Ma.: Affirmation Books, 1976), p. 80.
2. Eugene Kennedy and John Gorman, "Immaturity," *Living the Mature Priestly Life*, tape 3, (Chicago: Thomas More Assoc., 1975).
3. Everett L. Shostrom, *Man, The Manipulator*, (New York: Bantam Books, 1968), pp. 40-43.
4. Carl Rogers, "The Place of Feelings and Emotions," (Chicago: Instructional Dynamics Incorporated), *Mental Health Info-Pak Cassette Series*, Tape 2.
5. John Powell, *Why Am I Afraid To Tell You Who I Am?* (Chicago: Argus Communication, 1969), pp. 54-62.
6. John Powell, *The Secret of Staying in Love*, (Niles, Illinois: Argus Communication, 1974), pp. 80-81.
7. Bernard J. Bush, *Intimacy: Issues of Emotional Living In An Age of Stress For Clergy and Religious*, (Whitinsville, Ma.: Affirmation Books, 1978), pp. 48-51.
8. Francis J. McGuire, "Emotions, Conflict and Love," *Emmanuel Magazine*, May, 1974, p. 203.
9. John Powell, *Why Am I Afraid To Tell You Who I Am?*, *op. cit.*, pp. 79-84.
10. David Viscott, *The Language of Feelings*, (New York: Pocket Books Inc., 1976), p. 26.
11. John Powell, Why Am I Afraid To Tell You Who I Am? op. cit., pp. 65-77.
12. Thomas A. Kane, *The Healing Touch of Affirmation*, Whitinsville, Ma.: Affirmation Books, 1976), p. 79.
13. Willard Gaylin, *Feelings—Our Vital Signs*, (New York: Harper & Row, 1979), pp. 3-9.
14. John J. Malecki and Susanne Breckel, Sexuality: *The Celibate's Response*, National Assembly of Religious Brothers, Tape 3, (West Springfield, Ma.: Passionist Broadcasting, 1978).

CHAPTER FIVE

AUTHORITY

Several years ago I attended the blessing of a church by the local bishop. The clergy participating in the blessing were invited for dinner in the undercroft of the church after the ceremony. As usually happens when priests gather, small groups formed and camaraderie was quickly established. However, as the bishop entered the undercroft, the atmosphere quickly changed. The priests' voices became noticeably softer and there was an immediate movement to the various tables to prepare to eat. The pastor escorted the bishop to the head table, but no one chose to sit with them. So the bishop pleaded with some of his priests to join him for the meal. Reluctantly, a few slowly moved forward until the head table was filled. These priests did not want to sit with their bishop because they feared his scrutiny. They were uncomfortable with him. There was a certain distance between the bishop and his priests; there was no peership, no real rapport, no true friendship between them.

Feelings Toward Authority

Underlying these feelings of uncomfortableness with a person in authority are *feelings of fear* because the boss has power over us. She/he can transfer us from one position to another, can change our whole life by moving us from a city and people we love to a city 150 miles away where we know no one. Another reason for fearing authority is that we might feel that these persons in authority are only present to criticize us. Possibly this feeling exists because in the past affirmation came from superiors with great infrequency and criticism with frequency. Even many of our parents were not instructed how to affirm us as human beings, but rather how to correct and mold us to become obedient children.

Associated with these feelings of fear is *suspiciousness*. Some of us are constantly on guard for fear the boss will take advantage of us. He might give us more than our share of the work, might take a day off and leave hospital calls for us, might go to a banquet for lunch and eat prime rib while we eat hamburger. The superior attends workshops in Florida and California while we are limited to those within 300 miles. Beneath this suspiciousness is the idea that people in power always get the best by "using" their subordinates, resulting in an attitude of "we better look out for ourselves." One young priest who had this attitude always noted bitterly when his pastor got his haircut and took care of his personal banking needs on a day the pastor was supposed to be working. Naturally associated with these feelings of suspiciousness are feelings of anger toward authority.

Coping With These Feelings

Because we are uncomfortable in the presence of authority figures, often times we *either fight or flee them*. This is a very normal reaction. If we observe the major coping behaviors of the subhuman species whenever there is conflict between animals of the same species, we usually observe two patterns, the flight or fight response on the part of one of them. Both fighting and running away are very efficient ways for animals to deal with each other. These methods of coping seem to be almost automatic responses with great survival success in the lower animals. We fight and run from each other as human beings too, although this is not always done freely and openly. Most often it is done in ways that are disguised from each other. In spite of the fact that we have flight and fight in common with the lower animals, what distinguishes us from them is our verbal and problem-solving brain that has given us great superiority over the animals.[1]

Sometimes we flee authority by moving many miles from them. A priest happily takes a parish some distance from the main city in the diocese to escape the possible scrutiny of his bishop. A woman lay minister gladly offers to visit the shut-ins of the parish to avoid meeting frequently with the pastor as the director of religious education does. We seldom attend social gatherings and meetings when we know the superior will be present, unless we feel it's "a must." When we do attend, we try our best to avoid the person in authority, sitting far away from him.

Other times we fight constantly with authority. Possibly in every group there are one or two people who criticize every guideline the bishop or religious superior gives. These people are rebelling in general. They balk against religious and civil authority with equal venom. They join every march which attacks an "authority figure." In their immaturity, these persons rebel for the sake of rebelling and in this way are ventilating some of their pent-up hostility toward authority in general, like the high school student who expressed hostility toward authority by throwing a pie in the face of a teacher. Most often instead of engaging in a direct and constructive interchange, we fantasize an argument with a person in authority saying, "She should mind her own business." Or perhaps we use a more modern form "It's unfair because she doesn't practice collegiality." Another version of this modern argument is, "It's contrary to Vatican II because there is no shared decision making taking place."

A unique example of fleeing from authority occurred in an interpersonal group which I recently led. There were seven members and we were discussing the date of our next session, which had to be changed because of a holiday. One member said she could not make it on Wednesday and I said Tuesday was bad for me. Another member immediately urged the group to meet on Tuesday. This member made this suggestion because he feared authority as he said earlier "I don't like authority because they often take advantage of you. They boss you around too much." As the leader of the group, I represented authority for him and so he was anxious to have a session without me, to distance himself from me. At the same time, he seemed to be saying that the group didn't need any "authority," that in his life things would be better without any boss.

A danger that results from distancing ourselves from superiors is the fact that we easily become isolated. We become our own authorities since we don't interact with persons in authority or even our peers to confront us about decisions. We become a law unto ourselves, and no one ever challenges us because we clearly are "the boss." When we meet infrequently with superiors, they sense our uncomfortableness, insecurity and fear, and since they don't know how to handle that, they become uncomfortable. As a result, they don't seek us out, but rather allow us to maintain our distance from them and continue our non-constructive behavior.[2]

Another way of reacting to authority besides flight and fight is that of *total submission*. In early September of my first year of philosophy, the Archbishop ordered us to pray the litany of the saints every day after Mass for rain so that the crops would be good. Unfortunately, the dry August continued throughout the month of September. We kept on praying the litany of the saints daily until the middle of October when the Archbishop was finally asked if we could stop the litany. Even though I am not a farmer, I don't think rain in October would benefit the fall harvest after two rainless months. However, this decision could not be made on our own, but needed to be sought from the Archbishop. This kind of excessive dependence discourages the assumption of authority. It encouraged us to be completely obedient, conforming to every utterance that comes forth from any person in authority. It urged us to be extremely dependent, looking to authority for solutions to every problem. As a result, we thought very little on our own and always asked superiors many questions to avoid accepting responsibility for our own decisions. We never disagreed with authority, nor shared any of our own real feelings or opinions, but rather adopted their opinions as our own. This reminds me of the old priest who told a bishop shortly after his ordination to the episcopacy, "As a result of becoming bishop two things will take place, you'll never want for a meal and you will never be told the truth again."

This attitude is illustrated more clearly by referring to Lawrence Kohlberg's stages of moral development. His first stage is entitled punishment and obedience because it emphasizes avoiding punishment and unquestioning deference to power in their own right. His second stage might best be explained by the phrase, "you scratch my back and I'll scratch yours." At this time a person is interested mainly in satisfying one's own needs and occasionally the needs of others. Good intentions become important in the third stage in which good behavior is described as trying to please or help others. It's also important to earn approval by being "nice."[3]

When a person has successfully completed all three of these stages, then she/he can enter the fourth stage which we were describing earlier as total submission to authority. If we are in this stage, there is a tremendous emphasis on law. At this point there is an orientation toward authority, fixed rules, maintaining order in society, and doing our duty. We fear deviating from rules because that might lead to social chaos. Here we view our obligation to obey the law as more important than our obligations to our friends and groups. We sympathize with well-intentioned people who break the law, but our sympathy is overridden by our concern for keeping the social order which demands a strict adherence to rules and authority. There is no room for any autonomy in judgment, no possibility of using our own minds to decide what is right and wrong. We rely totally upon law and give blind obedience to it.[4]

In this phase of moral development, we tend to interpret the Bible very strictly and frequently refer to God as a law-giver rather than as a loving and merciful father. In our strict interpretation of the Bible we demand perfection of ourselves in order to be saved and do the same for others. In our reading of God's word we emphasize those passages where God punishes his people for their lack of obedience and other passages where he rewards people for adherence to the law. Damnation is frequently mentioned.

This type of total submission to authority recalls the Watergate Trial, when defendants stated they did not intend to violate any laws, but were only doing what they were told to do by their superiors. During the trial, the judge made it clear that people are not virtuous who obey commands blindly, but insisted that subordinates reflect on the commands given to them to make sure they are ethical and within the competence of those issuing them. The reaction of the general public indicated that they agreed with this, and that it is not sufficient for a person to be well-intentioned.

Sometimes this total submission expresses itself in a pastoral care program when students constantly quote their supervisor rather than expressing any of their own ideas. Other times it is displayed by insecure students who frequently praise their supervisor with the hope that this will win the acceptance of the supervisor which is needed badly to bolster a poor self-image. One religious woman interacted with me in that manner telling me, "You have great insight. You amaze me how much you know what's going on in a group. You really present interesting lectures too. I'm never bored. I put your ideas into practice and they always work with the patients too. You're simply amazing." I enjoyed the compliments and, at the same time, realized that they were coming from her need for my acceptance.

Source of Our Attitudes and Feelings

In order to mature in our relationships to authority, it is necessary to look at authority openly to consider how we acquired our present attitudes. A good place to begin is to reflect on our attitude toward our parents. While growing up, were we frequently threatened with punishment? Threatened to be sent to bed without our supper if we did not obey immediately? Threatened constantly of being deprived of new clothes or our privileges if we came home fifteen minutes after the curfew? Possibly some of us were reared in an atmosphere where we were frequently told, "Children should be seen and not heard." We were constantly reminded to respect our parents, a respect that caused fear and distance from them. In this atmosphere, no doubt there were times when we became not only fearful of our parents, but angry with them because they demanded perfection of us. Naturally, we could not measure up to their perfectionistic demands and consequently did not feel cherished, loved and valued.

On the other hand, maybe we were blessed to grow up in a home where we were often affirmed as a human being. We were loved and accepted just for being who we were, without any obligation to produce in order to gain approval. We were reared in a warm, loving atmosphere where our parents displayed their affection for us with many hugs and kisses, yet still grew up with an understanding of the meaning of "no." Such a person was Pope John XXIII. Because of the affirmation he received as a child, he was constantly affirming people in his life. Whether it was in personal contact or on television, young and old, Catholics and non-Catholics, all over the world were touched by Pope John's affirmation.

An example of his ability to affirm people occurred when he visited the inmates of Regina Coeli prison in Rome under a blue, cloudless sky. In his address to them he expressed his pleasure at the opportunity of visiting them and recalled for them that one of his cousins had once served a term in prison. He concluded his talk, "I have come. You have seen. I have looked into your eyes. I have placed my heart alongside your heart. Be assured that this meeting will remain deeply engraved in my heart." After his formal greeting, a few prisoners were permitted to approach him and kiss his ring. One of them, a murderer, looked at him with sad eyes and asked, ''Are those words of hope you have given me for such a great sinner as I am?'' In response, Pope John bent over the convict and embraced him.[5]

A beautiful example of an affirming person in my own life was Joe Emmanuel, a professor of counseling at Wright State University. I was one of eight participants in a growth group he was leading. At the beginning of each session, he asked us how we were working on our goals for personal growth. Because of an atmosphere of affirmation that he created, the persons were less hesitant to share their failures. Initially he affirmed persons in their struggles to grow, but after a short time the members supported one another, following his example. In other words, he was a catalyst in forming an accepting, affirming group of people who never knew each other before the group began.

Next, it is profitable to evaluate our *attitude toward God as an authority person*. How do we view God? Are we fearful of God because we look upon him as a person who is a just judge, a law-giver, one who rewards the good and punishes the evil? Do we look upon ourselves as being nothing in his presence, as abosulutely worthless? Another attitude toward God is feeling comfortable in his presence because he is a forgiving, loving Father who many times forgave the Jewish people when they turned their backs on him. He is a person who continually seems to give people another chance to love him, a person like Hosea who loves even an adulterous wife. Associated with this concept of God, is the idea that God has given us certain talents and gifts. He has blessed us with certain skills which he expects us to use. God loves us and that's why he gifted us.

Probably, our feelings toward our dads and our God are similar. After all, both of them are authority figures whom we call ''father.'' It's beneficial for us to re-examine these attitudes to see if we would like to change any of them. If we are uncomfortable being with authority persons, we might want to rid ourselves of fear toward them, rid ourselves of any ''tapes'' that demand perfection of us and consider whether we would like to claim peership with them as fellow adults.

Associated with this source of *our feelings toward authority is our self-image*. Often we don't feel comfortable in the presence of authority, or we fear them because we are insecure persons and so give them more authority over us than they actually have. We attribute perfection to them and worthlessness to ourselves. Those of us who feel this way might be classified as "pleasers" because we are constantly striving to please other people, to conform our lives at the expense of self-determination. We "pleasers" base our lives on being accepted and approved by others, especially those in authority and suffer guilt feelings when we fail to satisfy them. We consider the evaluations of others as the measuring stick of our self-worth, regardless of who we are or how many talents we possess, regardless of what accomplishments we have attained. Life is meaningless for us, unless people approve of us. However, when others accept us, that approval is often short-lived because we find it difficult to accept and sometimes, even impossible to believe. We tend to doubt the sincerity of compliments and constantly seek more signs of approval.[6]

One lady who was studying in graduate school for her doctorate in psychology was such a person. She was blessed with good intellect, an attractive personality and a high degree of natural beauty. However, her father, a farmer, thought that women ought to go to high school, get married, have children and take care of the home. Because of his strong emphasis on that role for women, he never affirmed her as intelligent or even as attractive in personality or appearance. So she did not believe in her own worth. Finally, one day in a group sensitivity session, a member became very angry at her saying, "I am damned tired of you rejecting my compliments. I feel that you are intelligent, that you are easy to get along with and you reject these statements. In effect then, you are saying that I am stupid or lying and I don't like either implication." This was a turning point in this young lady's life because from this time on she realized how much authority she allowed her father to have over her and how difficult it was for her to accept compliments. If a pastoral care person is going to function effectively, she/he must practice what is mentioned in the book *If You Meet the Buddha On the Road Kill Him*. There it indicates that all of us are pilgrims, all of us are equal, all of us have our own talents and insights, and no one should be placed on a pedestal, as far superior to us. In other words, the author is urging us to claim our own authority and our own giftedness.[7]

Another aspect of "pleasers" is that our lives are like a yo-yo, going up and down depending on how many compliments we receive. Naturally, if someone offers criticism, that causes us to become depressed for some period of time. Thus, we are like putty in the hands of other people, extremely dependent upon them for support.

Authority and Our Response

Sometimes in our idealistic way of looking at things, we fantasy a world in which there is no authority, in which there is absolute freedom for everyone. This is pure fantasy because throughout our lives there are persons in authority to whom we must report; *everyone is responsible to someone*; everyone has a boss. This is a fact of life. Even the president of our nation reports to Congress and is not totally free. Mr. Nixon and Watergate illustrated this clearly.

As human beings, God is an authority in our lives. Since he is our Creator, he has a right to establish commandments for us; he has a right to tell us how to live through the teachings and example of Jesus Christ in the gospels. As pastoral persons, an obvious authority is the Church and its leader, Pope John Paul II for Roman Catholics. His encyclicals and decrees as well as those of his offices in Rome demand our attention. Next, we have the bishop of our diocese along with his assistants in the chancery office. For many of us, there is a pastor or hospital ad- ministrator to whom we report. Finally, some of us have a parish council and parish commissions which demand our respect. In addition to these persons and commissions invested with authority, all of us have friends who have some authority over us. A friend is someone whom we trust, someone whose opinions are worthy of our consideration. We freely give that person some authority over us and in turn have some authority over him/her. There is a certain interdependence between us.[8]

Recognizing that all of us are responsible to someone and report to some authority (superior), *we now have the choice of responding or reacting to that person*. We can react to authority with uncomfortable- ness, fear, anger, a desire to escape, etc., or we can choose to respond by giving it an appropriate place in our lives. In responding to authority, we recognize that it does exist, but that it does have limits. In responding to authority, we know that authority does not have the power to control our whole lives, nor power to destroy us, however, it has power over certain aspects of our lives. Thus, persons in authority might demand that we change our lifestyle to some extent. We might be required to compromise some of our patterns of behavior or methods of functioning in a work situation. This compromise results, though, from an open and direct interaction with persons in authority where we feel comfortable enough to share our opinions and feelings and feel comfortable enough to listen to the feelings and opinions of our boss.

In other words, we feel comfortable with persons in authority. We are comfortable with God because we view him as a loving, merciful being who loves us so much that he made us to his own image and likeness. We regard God as a kindly Father who is interested in us and our welfare. We look upon God as one who values us so much that he gave each of us talents and gifts, and the greatest of all gifts, his own son, Jesus.

As mature individuals, we look upon human persons in authority not as our masters, but rather as persons who are trying to serve us. We regard the Pope as the "servant of servants" rather than a majestic superior to whom we must offer homage. We look upon superiors as those who assist in our growth, as those who assist us in fulfilling the will of God, rather than persons who have power over us. In the true sense of the word "authority" which has its roots in the word "author," the pastor or administrator is a developer, an enabler. A person in authority is like the author of a book, an originator, a designer, one who develops and brings the hidden reality into existence. Persons with structured positions of authority need to meditate often upon this concept so that they never use their authority as "power over people." An authority, like Jesus Christ, is one who enables, develops, helps design the possibility for the actualization of the potential of the persons entrusted to his care.[9]

In psychological terms, the purpose of authority is the ultimate development of self-direction and self-regulation so that an individual may live a resourceful and abundant life. The purpose of authority is not to control other people but rather to lessen control on others. Many individuals view authority as discipline which is interpreted as punishment or severe arbitrary restrictions imposed in order to punish or to teach someone a lesson. This notion is so common that the role of legitimate authority in leading the person towards self-regulation and self-direction is often ignored or repudiated when it is rightfully offered.[10]

Claiming Our Own Authority

It is important to recognize our own authority too. Part of the growth process in becoming effective pastoral persons is to claim our own authority. This means claiming rights that are ours as persons, claiming our Bill of Rights, the right to be treated with respect, the right to be listened to and taken seriously, the right to ask for what we want, the right to ask for information from other professionals, the right to have and express our own feelings and opinions, the right to choose not to assert ourselves, and the right to make mistakes.

When we fail to claim our own authority as pastoral persons, that affects our ministry. In introducing ourselves to patients in a hospital, some of us state clearly our authority. "I'm Sr. Marie, the chaplain of this unit." Others who are unsure of ourselves are very meek in our introduction, "I'm Sr. Jackie and I dropped by to see you," or 'I'm Mike Thoms, one of the students here in Chaplaincy program." In these last two examples, the persons did not assume their authority as chaplain of the floor.

Some of us indicate our comfortableness with ourselves by allowing the patient to take the conversation wherever she/he wishes, while others of us are anxious and display it by a need to control the conversation. We ask very direct questions frequently and thereby control the topics of the conversation. Our anxiety is further indicated by our need to speak all the time and never to permit brief silences which might allow the patient to reflect on what was said, or to introduce a significant topic.

It happens sometimes that we are too quick to refer people to other professionals. We refer to the head chaplain, the social worker or the nurse instead of ministering to the person ourselves. A patient asks a theological question, and immediately we feel our inadequacy in the matter and call for a theologian. A patient expresses feelings of depression, and we quickly excuse ourselves to call for a psychologist or social worker to help the patient. Often upset people speak to us about these matters because they like us and hope we will assist them, and not immediately send them to someone else. If we do decide to refer, then this is done with the person's knowledge and with the realization that someone more skilled than ourselves is needed.

Those of us who fail to claim our authority as professional chaplains, also tend to avoid certain topics. If the patient introduces the possibility of his dying, we might strive to reduce our uneasiness by switching the subject to a safe topic, the weather. However, when our identity and authority is certain, we are willing to walk through the valley of death with them and at their pace, not ours.

Finally when we claim our own authority in visiting the sick, we are aware of the valuable contribution we are making to their welfare. When a doctor or nurse interrupts our conversation without even excusing themselves, we let them know we are also professionals with specific skills to employ for the patient's benefit. This is often very difficult and a real test of our own authority because we tend in our culture to be overawed by the medical profession. There is the added difficulty in deciding an appropriate place to communicate to the medical person our displeasure at such discourtesy. One time when a doctor did this to me, I interrupted his conversation with the patient to introduce myself so that he knew I existed. Other pastoral persons have waited for the medical person outside the patient's room to convey their hurt and angry feelings. Each of us must choose for ourselves how to respond, but it is important to claim our own authority in some manner.

If without consulting us our pastor or administrator makes a decision which affects us, this presents another opportunity for claiming our rights as persons. As a person, we have a right to be consulted before a decision is made when that decision affects our work or life. Most leaders are happy to know that they have worked too fast and neglected to seek consultation appropriately.

Authority and Freedom

Naturally, there is tension between the authority of pastors or the chief chaplain and the freedom of other members of the pastoral team. Sometimes the leaders think that others are exercising too much freedom, while other times the pastoral people doing the field work think their leaders are abusing their authority by setting down too many rules. However, authority and liberty are twin sisters who cannot live without each other, and they need not be in conflict. After all, as we stated earlier, the function of authority is to guide others to their proper destiny. Authority in some persons is for liberty in others. So authority is harmonious with individual freedom; they are complimentary to one another, and not opposed.[11]

However, in reality there are times when struggles exist between them. Part of this is due to the fact that we are dealing with human beings. Another that there is a period of adjustment going on at the present time, with more freedom being given individuals than ever before. Our culture and the teachings of the Second Vatican Council are urging this. Presently there is a tendency to moderate the influence of external law and of authority in general, and to increase personal responsibility. It is beneficial to remember though, that freedom is not license, not the absence of all restraints, but rather the ability to do what one feels God is calling one to do. In the words of Pope Paul VI:

> "But at the same time, we must be conscious of the fact that our Christian liberty does not remove us from the law of God in the ultimate demands it makes on us in the realms of human wisdom, of evangelical spirit, of self control, of penance, and of obedience to the communitarian order proper to an ecclesial society. Christian liberty is not charismatic in the arbitrary sense that is claimed for it by some prophets of our time: St. Peter the Apostle teaches us to act as free men — not as men who make of liberty a camouflage for their malice, but as servants of God" (1 P 2:16).[12]

Freedom is the opportunity to choose, to select options. It includes the possibility of making mistakes, to say that we don't know the answer to that question. Freedom is to be real, to share ourselves with others, our strengths, our weaknesses even with superiors. Freedom means, with the help of God, to establish our own standards to measure ourselves by, rather than to adopt standards that are imposed by others. It means to follow our own informed consciences. It means to experience the love of others for one's self, to give love to others. Finally it means to value one's self as having worth.

To achieve an appropriate balance between authority and freedom it may be profitable to look at Paul's epistles when he stresses the importance of law and at the same time freedom of the sons of God, freedom of the spirit. Another helpful source to assist in achieving this balance may be assertive training groups which encourage self-expression, but with some concern for other persons. The first belief of many of these training groups is that we respect ourselves and others. This respect is shown by standing up for ourselves — expressing our thoughts, feelings and preferences and at the same time being mindful of the rights and feelings of the other person. The second belief urges us to be aware that life cannot be lived without hurting people from time to time. It's important for us to understand that other people are not so fragile they will be crushed

forever by something we do or say. We need to trust that other people
have a certain elasticity about them to bounce back from a hurt they might
receive. Besides, if we live fearing we might hurt someone, then we will
be paralyzed and unable to do anything. The third belief is that sacrificing
integrity and denying our own needs harms personal and community
relationships which are built only on trust and openness. As a result, we
keep our relatives and friends at arm's length and force them to guess how
they might assist us. Often too, they know something has upset us and
they waste a lot of time and energy trying to figure out what it was they
said or did that caused it. Where we share our needs and feelings openly
with others, it is much more loving. The final belief is that sacrificing our
own rights and needs teaches others to take advantage of us. On the other
hand, when we tell others how they affect us, this gives them a chance to
change and grow in their relationship to us and probably to other people
as well.[13]

Conclusion

There are four possible responses to authority by pastoral care
persons. First in our relationship to authority we can be very passive,
submitting ourselves totally to persons in authority. This means that we
never express our feelings, thoughts, or preferences. We limit ourselves
to occasional hints at them and often deny them. We make requests
indirectly, apologetically and even self-effacingly. Our body language is
"pardon me for living." Consequently, we violate our own rights as
human beings. Second, we respond to authority aggressively, demanding
our rights, forcing certain things to take place. With this attitude we stand
up for our rights, but we have no concern for the rights of others. We want
our own way no matter what we have to do to get it. We humiliate or
demean others in order to get what we want. Third, we respond to
authority in a passive, aggressive manner. We get what we want when we
want it, but we attain our goal in an indirect way. We are dishonest, make
others feel guilty and use sarcasm. We do not relate to our immediate
superior, but rather go to the personnel director or the bishop to obtain our
goal. At times we put on the "poor me" attitude and at other times give
people the silent treatment. We are a master at manipulation to attain our
goal.

Finally, as mature Christians, we are assertive in our behavior, expressing our thoughts, feelings and preferences clearly, and leaving the other person to respond or not. Here open communication is practiced. We respect ourselves and we respect other people. We stand up for our own rights, but we do not violate the rights of others. This requires honesty, humility and charity. It is risky. This kind of assertive behavior does not guarantee success in our relationships with authority and other people, but it certainly does increase the odds of relating effectively with them.

Footnotes

1. Manuel J. Smith, *When I Say No, I Feel Guilty* (New York: Bantam Books, Inc., 1975), p. 5.
2. James F. Campbell, "Priests, Authority and Growth," *Pastoral Life*, June, 1977, pp. 3-4.
3. Ronald Duska and Mariellen Whelan, *Moral Development*—A Guide to Piaget and Kohlberg, (New York: Paulist Press, 1975), pp. 45-47.
4. Ronald Duska and Mariellen Whelan, *op. cit.*, pp. 64-66.
5. Conrad W. Baars, *Born Only Once*, (Chicago: Franciscan Herald Press, 1975), pp. 45-46.
6. Joseph L. Hart, "Perils of the Pleasers," *Loneliness*, edited by James P. Madden, (Whitinsville, MA: Affirmation Books, 1977), pp. 45-50.
7. Sheldon B. Kopp, *If You Meet The Buddha On The Road Kill Him*, (New York: Bantam Books, Inc., 1976), p. 19.
8. James F. Campbell, *op. cit.*, p. 4.
9. Thomas A. Kane, "Coping With Community," *Coping: Issues of Emotional Living in an Age of Stress for Clergy and Religious*, edited by Bernard J. Bush, (Whitinsville, MA: Affirmation Books, 1976), pp. 24-25.
10. James J. Rue and Louise Shanhan, *Daddy's Girl, Mama's Boy*, (Indianapolis: The Bobbs-Merrill Company, Inc., 1978), pp. 31-33.
11. Donald DeMarco, "The Foundation of Morality and the Function of Authority," *Review for Religious*, Sept., 1978, p. 704.
12. Pope Paul VI, "Allocution of Pope Paul VI," Wednesday, July 9, 1979.
13. Robert E. Alberti and Michael L. Emmons, *Your Perfect Right*, (San Louis Obispo, CA: Impact Publishers, 1978), pp. 27-28.

CHAPTER SIX

ANGER

Being in the presence of a husband and wife who are in a heated argument is probably more embarrassing to us and to them than if we inadvertently discovered them in a passionate embrace. That's because we have been taught it's not proper to display anger. How did we come to regard anger as such an objectionable emotion? We were conditioned to have this attitude through our parental training, our religious education and our modeling of the significant adults in our lives.

Our conditioning began in our early childhood. As toddlers, we vented our anger through crying; later as small children, we resorted to temper tantrums which may have included kicking and biting. Our parents, no doubt, punished us for such behavior, and we received the message that anger is bad. As children, too, we sometimes teased or fought with our sister, and we were told, "That's your sister, don't hit her; you're supposed to love her instead of hitting her." Again we picked up the message that anger is bad. Religion teachers often emphasized the many things parents were doing for us as children and so urged us always to be loving and grateful to them. The underlying message was we could never be angry with them; there was no mention of the possibility of loving them and being angry with them at the same time.

Another important factor in our attitude toward anger was our modeling of our parents when they became angry. How did they handle their anger? We knew them well enough to know that certain things we did or the neighbors did, made them mad. We watched what they did with their anger. If they became enraged, we wanted to hide because of our fear of them, and at the same time we became fearful of the emotion of anger. If they ''sat on'' their anger, then we learned that repression was the way to handle anger.

Our difficulties in dealing with the emotion of anger were increased when our religion teachers taught us anger is sinful. In the Roman Catholic Church until recently, one of the questions we asked ourselves in our examination of conscience before confession was, ''Have I ever been angry?'' The clear message was that all anger is sinful, no matter how it was expressed. As we grew older, the religion teachers told us about Jesus becoming angry in the temple. The teachers concluded it was permissible to get angry, but there had to be a justifiable reason, like Jesus had when he drove the money-changers out of the temple with a whip. This didn't allow us many opportunities to become angry without sinning. Reflecting on that education today, it is difficult to understand how it could be given, considering the many other times in the Bible Jesus became angry. He was angry with the Scribes and Pharisees on a number of occasions and once was so angry he called them whited-sepulchers. Several times he was angry with his apostles because they could not understand he had to suffer and die before entering into his glory, even though he spoke clearly of a spiritual kingdom. Other times, he became angry with them because they were arguing who was going to be the greatest in his kingdom. An additional factor in our education concerning anger is that religious leaders held up the ''meek Jesus'' during his sufferings as the model to imitate. Pastoral care persons today are challenged to present the ''total Jesus'' as a model worthy of imitation, that is, Jesus who expressed not only his love and acceptance of the limitations of others, but his anger and frustration as well.

Sharing Our Anger

So our home and religious training in most cases instilled in us an attitude that makes us uncomfortable when we experience ourselves as angry, and especially uncomfortable when the anger is directed to our mother, father, good friend, spouse, or religious superior. An additional reason for our uneasiness is our fear that anger destroys relationships.

As ''don't make wavers,'' we fear anger kills the love we have for another and then ask ourselves how we could possibly live without love. Anger naturally makes waves and does kill this kind of neurotic love that depends on displaying 100% harmony. In reality though, this isn't love, but neurotic dependency which is confused with love. So, anger doesn't destroy healthy relationships, nor does it kill people. Rather, denying anger can result in the killing of relationships and people too and becoming angry and sharing angry feelings strengthens true love and actually affirms a relationship. A novice director, for example, shared her anger with a young nun for coming late for an appointment. At this the novice responded with some anger, telling her the circumstances causing her tardiness. Once their anger was shared with the reasons for it, they felt closer to one another realizing that in their open relationship it's O.K. to become angry with each other. Thus, it isn't anger that kills, but those people who are frequently divorced from all their feelings and unaware of their rage.[1]

Another aspect of the problem is dealing with ambivalent feelings, our feelings of love and anger or hate toward the same person. The old childhood messages of exclusiveness remain with us; we either feel love or anger, but not both simultaneously. As a result, we say to ourselves, "I love my friend, I want him to be my friend always so how can I be angry with him." We are confused by these ambivalent feelings, not believeing they are possible. In reality though, hate and love are not mutually exclusive, and it is possible for me to love my friend, but to be angry with him when he comes half an hour late for our golf outing. It's important for us to make anger serve love by integrating the two of them. This is done when we clean up our anger by enabling ourselves to fight with those whom we love. However, this fighting occurs in such a manner that there is respect for each other's vulnerable spots so that there is no hitting below the belt which causes the other person to feel overwhelmed. This means channeling our angry feelings so that they are released in a constructive way.[2]

Another aspect is the confusion of the meaning of anger. Today we hear a lot about "anger workshops" and "self-assertion workshops" as if they are the same. However, anger and self-assertion are different. Webster's New Collegiate Dictionary defines anger as "emotional excitement induced by intense displeasure." This definition describes a reaction, but it carries with it no judgments or predictions of loss of control. It simply identifies a reaction to intense displeasure. When we wish to communicate a loss of control, accompanied by destruction or pain, we have the words—fury, wrath, and rage to describe that. So anger workshops deal with identifying and channeling intense displeasure. Self-assertion workshops, on the other hand, enable shy people to feel the freedom to stand up for their own rights. Another word confused with anger is aggression which is sometimes associated with destruction. This causes us to reject anger as unacceptable to our image of a good Christian. Usually, though, destruction and loss of control result from anger that is unidentified.

Once we realize that anger is nothing but intense displeasure, then we are more readily able to own our anger. For example, we plan on taking a vacation for three months and have made all the arrangements, when the boss informs us our vacation is changed to another time; we are driving along the road at the speed limit and somebody behind us keeps blowing the horn, commanding us to go faster; we plan for several hours for a meaningful reconciliation rite for the whole parish and then only a handful of people show up for the service. These incidents and many others in our daily living are occasions for us to become angry which is as common as rain and sunshine. It's healthy for us to allow ourselves to feel our anger, realizing this is not something controllable to a large extent, but rather is part of our human nature. These feelings of anger are similar to feelings of a sexual nature. They are part and parcel of being a human being.

Constructive Use of Angry Feelings

From our experience we know we can't rid ourselves of these angry feelings by walking them away, by talking them away, by drinking them away, by smoking them away, nor by sleeping them away. So as pastoral persons we need to learn how to deal with them constructively in our own lives and to assist others to do the same. In handling all feelings effectively and in particular angry feelings, it is essential to realize we are having them. After identifying them, as mature adults we decide how we wish to express them, if we wish to express them at all. Since we are rational beings, our intellects come into play in determining the communication of our feelings. It is a choice we have as Christians. The question is not whether we become angry or not, but rather how and when do we share our feelings. Thus in dealing with anger effectively, there are three steps: identifying the feelings of anger, accepting these feelings as being part of our humanity, and then deciding the manner of expressing them, if that is our choice. The important thing is knowing and accepting angry feelings because this in itself mitigates against collecting and storing anger. Combining real acceptance of angry feelings without any judgment of them, along with the ability to express the anger, enables the person to have a choice regarding its expression.

In no way do I want to communicate the idea that sharing one's anger is something that takes a long time to decide, or that this method of delaying the expression of anger is the most effective manner of dealing with it. Rather the opposite is true. The most effective sharing occurs at the time we become upset. The longer we wait the less effective the message is, although sometimes circumstances dictate a delay or non-sharing of our anger. Besides, when there is a time lapse between the feelings of anger and the expression, then it is more difficult for the other person to recall the circumstances accurately surrounding the incident. Again, the strength of the message is dissipated.[3] So when a priest was fired from his position as hospital chaplain for a reason that seemed inadequate to him, it was far better for him to share his anger before leaving the hospital, rather than carrying his baggage as well as his pent-up anger.

Realizing that anger is an important aspect of our personality, it is easy to understand that our relationships are affected if we don't know how to deal effectively with it. We have difficulties at work relating to our co-workers, in the classroom being a good teacher who disciplines the students appropriately, at home being lovable and loving, and in religious life learning to express anger in such a way that effective changes take place. In other words, to establish good relationships at work, at play and at home, it is necessary to tell the person with whom we are annoyed, exactly what was said or done that was upsetting. An extremely important aspect of this sharing is to do it without blaming the other person, without saying you're wrong and I'm right. When we communicate our anger, our goal ideally is to share where we are, to inform the other person what's going on inside of us and not to condemn the other of wrong doing. For example, if a friend is late in picking me up, one approach is to criticize him all the way to the theatre about being the cause for us coming late to the movies. A more effective approach is to share my anger because it's important to me to see the very beginning of a movie and as a result of his coming fifteen minutes late, the movie will be started when we get there.

Anger Expressed in Our Bodies

It is easy for us to know when we are angry, because when this happens, we want to fight. Our whole system blasts this message home to us, and our bodies are prepared for action. Sugar pours into our system to enable us to have energy. More blood is circulated by increasing the blood pressure, and this makes the heart beat faster. More adrenalin is secreted to dilate the pupils of the eyes to enable us to see better and to help mobilize ourselves in general for action. If there is no release of this built-up energy, we remain in a constant state of readiness to fight, with heart beating rapidly, blood pressure elevated, and chemical changes occurring in the blood. It is clear the body can't withstand this for a long time. Something must give.

When our anger is unexpressed verbally, it often finds a way of expressing itself non-verbally through the body. A tension headache is a common manner. Our language even reveals the expression of this anger when we say "I'm going to blow my stack" and "I got to let off some steam." These phrases colorfully describe what's going on within us. Some people describe their tension headache as feeling like there is a very tight skull cap around their head. The pain which seems to go down the back of the neck is sometimes caused by a pinched nerve, but often by muscle tension which results from accumulated anger. This is clearly illustrated when we say, "He gives me a pain in the neck" because then we are accurately describing the situation.

In our everyday language we frequently hear the phrase, "I can't stomach that man." How accurate this phrase is, because it means I'm so angry I can't eat anything or accept anything into my stomach to digest. The digestive tract, a thirty foot long tube, is a very common outlet for the emotions when they cannot be expressed in other ways. Some people choose to express their emotions at the end of the tract, the colon. It's easy to recall some vulgar phrases we have in English to communicate our anger which include some mention of the products of the bowel. Some people merely use the vulgar phrases, but others develop diarrhea or constipation. This can be traced to our infancy when bowel movements had many meanings. For example. a bowel movement sometimes was a means of pleasing our parents and thereby getting their approval, or when we got angry at them, we soiled our clothes as a safe manner of sharing our anger. Possibly, this caused them to be embarrassed or at least, put them to the trouble of cleaning us.

Another common phrase in our language which indicates our bodily expression of anger is, "Don't get your blood pressure up" and "Watch out you'll blow a gasket." Again, this describes what is happening when we become angry; our bodies are prepared to fight and as a result, our pressure rises. If we don't resolve the anger, then the high blood pressure condition continues, and this results in chronic hypertension. A young executive, for example, who is consistently given more work by his boss, becomes very angry because of the excessive workload, but never shares his anger for fear it will hinder his chances of getting a promotion. As a result of his unreleased anger toward his boss, he has high blood pressure constantly and develops chronic hypertension.

The body can also express repressed anger through excessive overeating. This may have developed in early childhood when our parents punished us for the manner in which we ventilated our anger, e.g., kicking the furniture, and unfortunately we got the message, we were unlovable. In order to soothe that feeling, we eat more than usual. As we became adults, we continued to cope with anger by substituting feelings of being bad and unlovable. This naturally resulted in feelings of guilt and depression. We satisfied both of these feelings by overeating, and this overeating both punished and comforted us. The ultimate result of this pattern was overweight for us.

Other bodily ailments that commonly are associated with repressed anger are: vomiting, ulcers, respiratory illness, skin diseases, genito-urinary tract diseases, strokes, tics, heart attacks, depression, self-imposed starvation and either excessive sleeping or insomnia.[5]

In their personal lives pastoral care people need to learn how to deal with their anger in a healthy manner so that they themselves don't become sick by expressing it through their bodies. In addition, they learn the skill of eliciting the repressed anger of others so that they can become productive Christians, instead of people weighed down by avoidable illness. When some persons are hospitalized, they get in touch with their pent-up anger and so welcome assistance in relieving themselves of this poisonous venom.

Hostility, Passive Aggressiveness and Displacement

Our bodies are not the only way our repressed anger is expressed. Hostile comments are another unhealthy manner and the unfortunate aspect about it is that we do not admit our remarks have a barb attached to them. When someone confronts us about our hostility, we deny having made the remark or suggest the person is paranoid for such an interpretation. One lady used to hide her hostility toward her husband with a lot of verbage; she told many stories, but had the uncanny habit of interjecting them with comments about widowhood, husbands dying and insurance policies. She simply could not understand why her husband became irritated when she did this. Another type of hostile person is the one who constantly finds one flaw in everything whether it is a plan, a painting, a house, etc. This kind of person, who might be called the ''but person,'' also does not admit any hostile intent. Some typical statements of this nature are:

''That homily was good, but too long.''

''The parish council really works hard, but it's a shame they accomplish so little.''

''That chaplain is really dedicated to the sick, but he's a workaholic.''

When others become angry at him for these hostile remarks, he is completely surprised and defends himself saying, ''I'm only being honest. You can't get angry at me for being truthful.'' Actually people are angry at him for his dishonesty, for his disguised anger.

Some other people are more open with their hostility, but still manifest their anger in a distorted fashion. An excellent example of this occurs in the play *Who's Afraid of Virginia Wolf.* The husband and wife enjoy cutting each other down in the presence of other college professors and their spouses. Everyone knows they are angry with each other, but they never share their anger directly. Instead, they take turns belittling each other, pointing out real and imaginary limitations. Their relationship could deepen if they spoke about their anger and its causes openly.

A devastating hostile expression is to deny the existance of the feeling of another. This hurts deeply because it directly contradicts the other person in the vulnerable area of feelings. This occurs on vacation when a person expresses his fear of climbing to the top of a mountain and his irritated friend responds, ''No, you don't. You get a kick out of being up on high ledges." If this happens often it tends to make a person crazy.

When a person accumulates a lot of anger, he may turn the anger in on himself and thus become depressed. This depression manifests itself by insomnia, poor appetite, feelings of hopelessness etc. If this depression becomes acute, the person feels worthless, blames himself for everything that goes wrong, and in extreme cases commits suicide, the ultimate of hostile actions. It is estimated there are about 25,000 suicides annually, but many suicides are never recorded as such. Not only are deaths reported as accidents when they are really intentional, but some persons are unaware they are committing suicide. Sometimes it is pointed out to a reckless driver, "You're trying to kill yourself driving like that and some day you'll succeed." We can only guess at the number of people who die in automobile accidents, boating and swimming accidents and drug overdoses because of their basic wish to kill themselves. Such a drive exists in a number of drug addicts and alcoholics. We describe the alcoholic as "drinking himself to death," while the same drive may be more subtle in the obese person who is "eating himself to death."[6]

Another unhealthy method of expressing our repressed anger is through passive actions or comments. Recently, I caught myself doing this playing golf. When a twosome playing behind us became impatient at our slow pace, they played constantly on our heels and then asked to play through us. I was angry with them and didn't want to wait for them to hit through us but reluctantly agreed. My passive aggressiveness was displayed when I left my golf cart in the middle of the fairway so that one of their balls might hit it and thus hinder their game. Another familiar manner of being passively aggressive is to refuse to listen to someone with whom we are upset. We can do this gently by simply reading the paper or watching the TV instead of lending the other person our ear.

Many other common ways of expressing passive aggressiveness are: not listening to another by talking excessively about a safe topic, looking bored, falling asleep on another, giving a person "the silent treatment," forgetting a person's name, speaking to another person in a group and avoiding one person whom you do not like, not looking at another when speaking to him, refusing to say hello to another in passing him in the hall or on the street, being unresponsive in sexual relations and withdrawing from another person emotionally. Possibly the most frequent hostile communication to the clergy happens during the homily on Sunday mornings when some people constantly are looking at their watches or reading the Sunday bulletin.

Some people are unable to share their anger with the person at whom they are angry and so they blast some other innocent person. A religious sister who is angry at her coordinator might fear expressing it and so takes it out on another sister who simply disagrees with her. This is called displacement because the anger is on another rather than on the real target. In this situation the person feels some release of the anger, but it is extremely ineffective because the person is often unaware of the real source of her feelings. It is more beneficial to share the anger with the person with whom we are angry; if that is impossible, the next best thing is to discuss the anger with a friend who is willing to understand us.

Pastoral care persons possibly are most tempted to avoid sharing their anger at their bishop, president of a religious community, pastor or chief chaplain. They are tempted to let their anger out by ''forgetting'' to accomplish a task on time, making a ''digging'' remark to the person in the position of authority, or blasting the secretary for minor mistake instead of sharing their anger with their boss. Naturally these kinds of behavior hinder their ministry.

Some of us by our temperament tend to use these maladaptive forms of sharing our anger more than others. Some tend to become angry very quickly, being natural fighters or hawks. On the other hand, there are others who are doves, that is, by nature they are not inclined to fight and don't like loud voices, shouting and yelling. A dove is likely to brag he's never had a fight, and when two doves marry, they proudly proclaim on their twenty-fifth wedding anniversary to all their relatives and friends, that they haven't had a fight or been angry with each other in twenty-five years of marriage. It's beneficial for us to realize whether we tend to be hawks or doves, but at the same time to realize there is no person who has never been angry. Hawks, in their extreme form, are bullies; they are always pushing people around and so are considerd impolite or boorish. Doves, on the other hand, in denying their anger appear as nice guys and nothing seems to upset them. As a result though, such persons take all the garbage that comes down the street. Their only overt response is a smile, but their covert responses are hostility, passive aggressiveness, displacement and depression.

One hospital chaplain didn't use any of these maladoptive forms when she became very upset with the chief chaplain who made a decision which affected her work, without consulting her first. She tried to visit patients, but gave up because she simply couldn't listen to them, since her whole being was absorbed with her anger at the chief chaplain. Later that afternoon she functioned effectively with the patients, after she demanded a brief meeting with her boss in which she shared her anger and the reason for it. Thus for anyone to minister effectively in a parish, hospital or nursing home setting, it is essential that the person have the freedom to experience his/her anger, accept it and decide how to express it appropriately.

Examples of Expressing Anger

Having discussed constructive and non-constructive methods of expressing anger in general, it's time to provide detailed examples of them. The situation is this: Bob and Carl, both priests, have been taking vacations together for years, but this year Bob decides he's going to Europe with a group of his parishioners. Bob, who meets people easily and mingles well in a crowd, doesn't tell Carl for fear it will hurt his feelings. But Carl, who is shy, sensitive and rather introverted, finds out about his plans through one of Bob's parishioners. Naturally, Carl is hurt and doubly so because of the manner in which the information came to him.

Carl calls him about the time for their weekly golf game and Bob begins to excuse himself.

Bob: "Gee, I'd love to go; the weather is going to be nice, but I have a graduation Mass tomorrow night and haven't given a thought to the homily yet. So I better cancel out for this week."

Carl: (Thinks: if you'd spent time on the weekend on that homily you could go. After all, you knew about the graduation Mass for a month).

Says: "I understand, but I'm surprised you put things off until the last minute like this."

Bob: (Thinks: who asked him to criticize my work habits. After all, this is a big parish, not a small-time operation like his).

Says: "I'm really sorry, but this is a large class and I really want to give them a good thought this year, instead of something just off the top of my head."

Carl: (Thinks: that dirty rat, he's going to mess up my vacation this summer and now the golf for this week too).

Says: "Well, if you can't, you can't. How long have you known about the graduation?"

Bob: (Thinks: he's nagging me just like my father did).

Says: "Hey, are you offering me unnecessary advice?"

Carl: (Thinks: I guess he doesn't want to be around me any more. He prefers the rich in his parish and the other priests who are big shots).

Says: (sarcastically) "I had no idea how important your graduation was to you this year."

Bob: (responding to the sarcasm) "Maybe the sun doesn't rise and set on those kinds, but they are important to me. After all, I've known most of them for five years now."

Carl: (Thinks: he's getting angry, I'd better cool it).

Says: "Why don't we forget the whole thing, even forget I called you. O.K.?"

Bob: Says: "O.K., I'll see you later."

It's obvious that interaction was not effective and so now I will have the same interaction, but with a real meeting of the two persons. Carl calls again about the weekly golf game.

Bob again begins to excuse himself:

"I'd love to, but I can't because I need to spend time preparing the homily for the graduation Mass tomorrow night.

Carl: "You know, that really upsets me. I was planning on a nice golf game to help me relax.''

Bob: I can understand that because I know you don't like to play alone and now you have nothing to do tomorrow.''

Carl: "Besides that, I heard from one of your parishioners, you're not going on vacation with me this year. I heard you're going to Europe with a group from your parish. I feel left out in the cold.''

Bob: "O.K. I guess you do.''

Carl: "And what makes it worse is that you never told me yourself, but I had to find out from someone else. This makes me angry because I thought we were really good friends.''

Bob: "I apologize. I was wrong. I should have told you about the vacation, but I didn't. I can see why you're mad at me.''

Carl: "Well, O.K., at least you understand.''

Bob: "Yes, it was my fault, but I want you to know that I do care about you and consider you a close friend.

Carl: "I'm happy to hear that.''

Bob: "I have cleared my calendar for next week and have the whole day off. How about if we splurge and play 18 at the country club and take a cart too.''

Carl: "O.K., that'll be good."

Bob: "I'm sorry about the golf tomorrow and the vacation for the summer too. Maybe we could take a week's vacation after I return from Europe."

Carl: "O.K. Let's talk about it more next week. Goodbye."

In the first example (the non-constructive expression of anger) there was no real meeting of Carl and Bob because the issue seemed to be Bob's procrastination. However, the real issue was the hurt and angry feelings Carl was experiencing because he was left out of Bob's vacation plans and the weekly golf outing. Associated with this was the issue whether Carl was a close friend of Bob's or not. In the "good fight" these feelings were clearly communicated and when Bob acknowledged them, Carl felt much closer to him. Thus, their relationship deepened. In the first example too, an unwritten rule or "family secret" is followed: we won't be honest with each other. The two friends share their anger through hostile remarks and passive aggressiveness. Obviously their relationship remains somewhat shallow and could be broken entirely if one or the other person no longer tolerated the unhealthy methods of sharing anger.

From such an interchange we can conclude three things about a constructive expression of anger. First, it is interpersonal communication. It deepens the relationship because it gives both parties a new awareness of the attitude and feelings of the other. It not only facilitates unclogging future communication gaps, but also increases each person's sensitivity. Second, it facilitates change. It attacks the present method of sharing with each other and lays the groundwork for new and more acceptable forms of relating. Third, it is informative. Correct details and feelings that formerly were lost or ignored are shared for each person to clearly understand. Often we tend to conceal or distort facts and feelings during an ineffective expression of anger.[7]

Forgiveness and Reducing Our Anger

While I urge expressing anger openly, anger over a particular issue ought to end at some point. We know this has happened when we have forgiven the other person. However, if we find it hard to forgive and forget, if we carry grudges after we have apparently resolved an issue, it would be profitable to determine what we get out of protracted resentment.

Some people maintain their anger out of a sense of moral righteousness or power, while others do this to avoid a sense of loss or pain. For example, a person who avidly supports abolishing capital punishment may maintain a righteous anger at anyone who disagrees with his high value of a human life. By encouraging anger at his opponents, he feels that he is an outstanding Christian. In divorce proceedings a wife might allow her anger at her husband to reach the point of rage in order to escape facing the reality that she is no longer a married woman.

When one pastoral person says to another, "Drop Dead," she doesn't really want the other person to die, but wants him to drop dead for a little while. This is the same as saying "drop dead as long as my anger lasts," which could be ten minutes. When our anger continues, when it keeps feeding itself, when the flame constantly flares up again, there is something wrong.[8]

Sometimes priests or sisters, active in pastoral work, agree that it's best to ventilate anger, but feel "tied up in knots" with the anger they experience toward the former rector of a seminary or novice mistress who made them feel they were the scum of the earth. What can these angry people do after all these years? The former director is now elderly and would never understand what the anger was all about. So what benefit is there in sharing the anger with that person? The significant aspect of this problem is for the priests or sisters to experience the anger and have the ability to convey it. As a result, they have a choice about sharing feelings. When one priest came to this point, he no longer felt the need to tell the former superior "where to go." The important change that took place within him was that he was in command and could decide for himself, because he was no longer a stranger to his own feelings. In addition, the priest realized that, even though the former rector's methods were terrible, he was doing what he thought was best with the knowledge of psychology available to him at that time. Thus, some reconciliation was achieved.

A natural effect of experiencing our anger, accepting and expressing it is to bring it to a conclusion. The opposite is also true: an effect of not allowing ourselves to feel our anger is to encourage it to keep simmering and periodically to burst into flames. So sharing our anger has the effect of reducing it.

We can also reduce our anger or the frequency of the times we become angry by limiting or reducing our expectations of perfection in ourselves or others. Frequently we become angry with ourselves because we don't meet the unreal goals which we establish for ourselves and others. We demand perfection and become upset when that is not attained. So, it is profitable for us to reexamine our expectations of ourselves and others to see whether they are realistic. Sometimes a chaplain becomes angry with a dying patient because she avoids the topic of death and switches the subject to the nurses' failure to answer her light sooner. A valuable question for the chaplain to ask himself is, ''I wonder why she switches the topic to anger at the nurses?'' and ''Is she discussing her death with someone else?'' By reflecting on his expectations he can determine whether they are real or not, and can reduce the frequency of his anger or frustration in working with the patients and the staff too.

A final method of reducing our anger is to share our expectations with others. Sometimes we assume other people know what we want done and what our preferences are, but our assumptions are not valid. We can save ourselves aggravation if we take the time to share our expectations with our fellow-workers or the people with whom we are living.

Music was used in the Old Testament by David to quiet Saul's nerves. Our modern rock and roll with its loudness and speed does not quiet us, but rather stirs up our anxiety level and angry feelings. It's good to be aware that constant listening to this type of music keeps us and others in a state of excitement and fosters the violent expression of anger. Movies that are excessively violent tend to have the same effect because they present the actors as models for us to imitate. We not only imitate their style of dress, etc., but also their violent expression of anger. Violent movies can, though, serve the function of assisting us in expressing our anger vicariously, if at the end of the movie it's clearly stated that this expression of anger is a substitute for ventilating our own anger and that we are not to model our lives after the actors in all aspects.[9]

Anger in Children

Children usually do not have the same problems as adults with anger because they are naturally aggressive and express their anger without shame. This is exemplified when they draw violent scenes with their crayons and when they play cops and robbers. Today children are taught to be possibly more expressive of their anger than in the past because they see more violence on TV. It is easily agreed that sixty to seventy percent of the news on the newscast is violent and indirectly the children are then taught that destructive violence is the way to solve problems, e.g., the terrorist groups killing officials of various countries as a means of rebelling against the present social system. When children watch a great deal of television, they easily pick up the idea that violence is a way of life, but unfortunately they are never taught how to release their anger except through violence. These young people, then, are in a similar bind to persons forty years ago in regard to their sexuality. At that time, they were not permitted to admit they had sexual feelings and so these feelings were repressed. Fortunately, our attitudes toward our sexuality have improved immensely and now we need to change our attitudes toward anger. We need, then, to admit to ourselves and teach to our children that it is O.K. to be angry but that we must channel it. It does not take a genius to understand that since kids watch so much violence on television and in motion pictures, that they have learned to ventilate their anger through destruction of property. This destruction increases unless pastoral people teach them it's O.K. to be angry but that the anger needs to be expressed constructively. It is necessary to help children become aware of their angry feelings, so that they experience themselves being angry and then can choose how they wish to share that.

Conclusion

It is my experience that pastoral care persons function effectively only if they are comfortable with their own anger and with other peoples' anger. If they repress their anger, possibly at God, when they see a young father of three children dying, then their anger might express itself by some bodily ailment or by helping the patient repress his anger toward God. If chaplains are unable to deal with their anger when some doctor intrudes on their visits with patients, they could become depressed and think about terminating their career in chaplaincy because it seems so insignificant when compared to the profession of medicine. One chaplain dealt effectively with his anger in such a situation by talking to the doctor later and ventilating his anger, saying that courtesy demands the doctor at least excuse himself before he interrupts a chaplain's visit. Sometimes patients are very angry because sickness has disrupted their plans. A pastoral person needs to encourage the expression of this anger rather than discouraging it by some pious platitude, "Everything works out for the best." A pastoral person ministers effectively with children when she/he seeks to interpret the anger expressed in drawings, instead of urging them to draw "nice" things. The same is true for those patients who are furious at the nursing staff for their cold, inefficient care. This kind of patient is assisted best by the chaplain who doesn't defend the staff, but rather listens as the patient ventilates his feelings and shares his viewpoint of his hospitalization. Pastoral people who fear anger might avoid such patients instead of helping them unburden themselves of their pent-up feelings.

Another aspect of our ministry is to teach people to model the whole Christ who was meek on some occasions and shared his anger freely on others. It's important for us to encourage that sound theology be taught in catechism classes, from the pulpit and in the sacrament of reconciliation concerning anger. It's beneficial for us to model constructive expression of anger by being as comfortable as possible with other people's anger and comfortable enough with our own to experience it, accept it and decide how to communicate it appropriately.

Footnotes

1. George R. Bach and Herb Goldberg, *Creative Aggression* (New York: Avon Books, 1974), pp. 39-49.
2. George R. Bach and Peter Wyden, *The Intimate Enemy* (New York: William Morrow, Inc., 1969), p. 386.
3. Theodore Isaac Rubin *The Angry Book* (New York: Macmillan Co., 1970), pp. 165-7.
4. Jane Templeton "Get Angry!" *Weight Watchers* (April, 1978), pp. 10-12.
5. Nancy Shiffrin, *Anger: How To Use It* (Chatsworth, A: Major Books, 1976), pp.32-44.
6. Leo Madow *Anger How to Recognize and Cope With It* (New York: Charles Scribner's Sons, 1972), pp. 87-90.
7. Jane Templeton "Get Angry" *Weight Watchers* April, 1978), pp. 10-12.
8. Nancy Shiffrin *Anger: How to Use It* (Chatsworth, A: Major Books, 1976), pp. 13-14.
9. George R. Bach "You are Aggressive" *Constructive Aggression* (Chicago: Human Development Institute, 1970).

CHAPTER SEVEN

SEXUALITY

Sexuality is part of ministry, just as it is part of every aspect of life. God made us sexual beings, and when we are ministering, we relate to others as sexual persons. We can't relate as "things" or only through our ministerial roles because then we fail to communicate our warmth and compassion. It is important that we pastoral persons are aware of our sexuality and are comfortable with it as we engage in ministry.

The opening paragraph of the document *Declaration on Certain Questions Concerning Sexual Ethics* published in 1976 by the Sacred Congregation for the Doctrine of the Faith, gives us a beautiful approach to sexuality. It states, "The human person is profoundly affected by sexuality, that it must be considered as one of the factors which give to each individual's life the principal traits that distinguish it. In fact, it is from sex that the human person receives the characteristics which on the biological, psychological and spiritual levels, make that person a man or a woman, and thereby largely condition his or her progress towards maturity and insertion into society."

The Meaning of Sexuality

These ideas certainly broaden our concept of sexuality. Formerly, whenever the word sexuality was used, it was restricted to genital sexuality. Now with the new concept of sexuality, our concept is broadened so that it will include four aspects: generation of children, relationships, sensual pleasure and fidelity.

In the first story of creation, Almighty God made everything including human beings and then concluded his creation by saying, "Be fertile and multiply, fill the earth and subdue it."[1] Here we have the generational aspect of sexuality.

The second chapter of Genesis states that after God created Adam, Adam was lonely because no one was like himself. He liked the animals, he enjoyed the beautiful scenery with its greenery, but he had no one equal to himself, no one with whom he could really communicate. So the Lord God said, "It is not good for the man to be alone. I will make a suitable partner for him."[2] When Almighty God brought Eve to Adam, Adam said, "This one, at last, is bone of my bones and flesh of my flesh. This one shall be called 'woman,' for out of 'her man,' this one has been taken."[3] This account illustrates the *relational aspect* of sexuality.

In the "Song of Songs" book of the Bible we have another aspect of sexuality, the *erotic and sensual*. The Song of Songs gives us an image in some detail of physical love and recognizes the sacredness of that love. Here we see a lover expressing feelings for the beloved which are erotic, human, passionate and sensuous. Specifically the author begins the book saying:

> "Let him kiss me with the kisses of his mouth. More delightful is your love than wine. Your name spoken is a spreading perfume; that is why the maidens love you. Draw me. We will follow you eagerly."[4]

Later on the author begins to become more specific in extolling the virtues of his beloved:

> "Your lips are like a scarlet strand, your mouth is lovely. Your cheek is like a half-pomegranate behind your veil. Your neck is like David's tower girt with battlements; a thousand bucklers hang upon it, all the shields of valiant men. Your breasts are like twin fawns, the young of a gazelle that browse among the lilies. Until the day breathes cool and the shadows lengthen, I will go to the mountain of myrrh, to the hills of incense."[5]

Finally, the woman speaks of the charms of her loved one in these words:

> "My lover is radiant and ruddy; he stands out among thousands. His head is pure gold; his locks are palm fronds, black as the raven. His eyes are like doves beside running waters, his teeth would seem bathed in milk, and are set like jewels. His cheeks are like beds of

spice with ripening aromatic herbs. His lips are red blossoms; they drip choice myrrh. His arms are rods of gold adorned with chryso-lites. His body is a work of ivory covered with sapphires. His legs are columns of marble resting on golden bases. His stature is like the trees on Lebanon, imposing as the cedars."[6]

There is little discussion of sexuality in the gospels, but it is discussed indirectly in Matthew's gospel when he speaks about divorce. Here there is strong emphasis on *fidelity*, and divorce is frowned upon because it is opposed to this fidelity. When a marriage takes place, the two people are no longer two, but one as a result of God's activity. Once this sacred relationship is created, it cannot be undone. This fidelity is likened to God's fidelity in his love for mankind. Even though mankind has been periodically unfaithful to God, God has never been unfaithful in his love for him. So the relationship between God and his people is similar to the relationship between a wife and a husband in marriage. The fidelity that God has displayed for his people is the same fidelity expected between a wife and a husband.[7]

Thus, sexuality has four components to it, it is not co-extensive with genitality, but with personality and the whole person. It is not something added to our humanity as if it is something extra, nor is it one component among many others of our human nature.[8] It is a deep mysterious aspect of personality; it is part of our total personhood. Possibly the strongest indication of this is that the first aspect we observe about others is that they are men or women; that is, we observe the sexuality of the other. Associated with that is the fact that the last thing we remember about others is not their name or occupation, but their sex, that is, we remember whether we related to a woman or a man.[9]

Particular Characteristics of Men and Women

If we look at sexuality from another viewpoint, it has four dimensions, the genital, the affective-social, the masculine and the feminine. In addition to genitality, sexuality includes our attractions for others, our relationships, our ability to be compassionate, tender, affectionate, and warm. Closely connected with these qualities are the characteristics which our culture ascribes to masculinity and femininity. As a result of cultural heritage, we think of men as authoritative, unemotional, logical and independent, and of women as submissive, emotional, nurturing and dependent. These so-called masculine and feminine qualities are not really genetically tied to any particular sex. There is nothing wrong with men being loving, tender and warm, or with women being assertive and taking initiative. It is good if both men and women are strong and weak, both assertive and gentle.

The fathers of the Second Vatican Council were sensitive to the changes of sex roles in various societies and were careful to avoid assigning any characteristics to one particular sex. In their *Pastoral Constitution on the Church in the Modern World* they always address ''spouses and parents,'' without designating special roles to husbands and wives, fathers and mothers. Marriage is described as an intimate union where a woman and a man are ''joined to one another in equal affection, harmony of mind and the work of mutual sanctification.'' The Church no longer speaks of man as the head of the home and the woman as the heart of the home.

As a result of cultural learning, we tend to attribute certain characteristics to men and others to women; men seem to have been encouraged to compartmentalize their experiences and to be task-oriented, while women have been encouraged to centralize and integrate their experiences. For example, if a husband and wife have argued most of the day and the arguments are unsettled at bedtime, the wife is less inclined to have sexual relations than the husband, who differentiates, in this case, the tense day and sexual relations. A woman more often than a man seeks to unify sex and love, she wants to integrate them. She usually seeks signs of love before she engages in sexual relations.

Men more easily and frequently dissociate their experiences; they tend to put their experiences in various categories. They also seem more likely to put everything aside while they involve themselves in an experience. They further tend to be more task-oriented and more distant from all their experiences—from the totality of their experiences. As a result, men have greater difficulty integrating their experiences than women generally do. For example, men are not as likely to look for love in genital relations and more easily separate love and sex. Some men find it very easy to treat women as sex objects, to treat them almost completely in physical terms. Men can dissociate their physical sexuality from the rest of the total person. Women also can treat men as sex objects, but not as readily. They tend to view men in their totality. This does not mean in any way that men are better than women or vice-versa; it simply means these tendencies exist.[10]

Early Attitudes Toward Sexuality

As it was indicated in the opening quotation, the attitude of the Church has changed in recent years regarding sexuality. It has changed through the centuries of its existence too. The biblical concept of sexuality as we noted earlier, is one of goodness and fellowship, generation, sensuous love and fidelity. The Gospels portray the affective dimension of sexuality when they describe Jesus as a compassionate, gentle, warm, tender and loving person. Paul in his Epistles speaks positively, but cautiously, about sexuality. He is positive in the sense that he likens the union of husband and wife to that of God and his people. This gives the relationship of woman and man in marriage a certain dignity. He is cautious because he expresses as a personal opinion that celibacy is to be preferred to marriage. Here he goes further than Matthew who says that both marriage and celibacy are viable options. Paul makes it clear that Jesus did not prefer one over the other, but that he does do so in expressing a private opinion. In his letter to the Corinthians, Paul adds that sex is dangerous because it has led some of them to sin. Further, noting the dangerousness of sex, he urges them not even to mention sins of sexuality.

St. Augustine in the fourth century expressed another approach to sexuality which was influenced by his Manichean past. He taught that physical pleasure is sinful and that all sexual intercourse must be procreative. In more detail, he listed a hierarchy with respect to sexual life stating that celibacy or sexual abstinence is excellent, procreative sexual intercourse in marriage is permissible, sexual intercourse in marriage for other reasons besides procreation is venially sinful, and sexual intercourse outside marriage is mortally sinful. These opinions of Augustine are a definite break from the biblical teachings.[11]

In succeeding centuries the view of Augustine was corrected, but generally the teaching of the Church on sexuality has been cautious and not extremely positive. Pope Pius XII in 1951 cautioned spouses about excesses in sexuality due to irrational passion when he taught married couples that ''as in eating and drinking, so in the sexual act, they must not abandon themselves without restraint to the impulse of the senses.'' This papal teaching as well as a number of others was rooted in the former common teaching that mankind lost perfect control of all the appetites as a result of the original sin of Adam and Eve. It naturally followed that our attitude toward genital sexuality and toward sensual pleasure ought to be one which emphasized control. As a consequence, we tended to think of sexuality as in terms of an instinct placed in our human nature by God which was difficult to control because of original sin and which must be carefully held in check at all times. In other words, we feared our sexuality, lest it would get out of control.[12]

Modern Attitudes Toward Sexuality

Since Vatican II, the attitude toward sexuality and love has changed appreciably. In *Humanae Vitae*, Pope Paul VI states:

> This (married) love is first of all fully human, that is to say, of the senses and of the spirit at the same time. It is not, then, a simple transport of instinct and sentiment, but also, and principally, an act of free will, intended to endure and to grow by means of the joys and sorrows of daily life, in such a way that husband and wife become one only heart and one only soul, and together attain their human perfection.
> Then, this love is total, that is to say, it is a very special form of personal friendship in which husband and wife generously share everything, without undue reservations or selfish calculations. Whoever truly loves his marriage partner loves not only for what he receives, but for the partner's self, rejoicing that he can enrich his partner with the gift of himself.

This positive attitude toward sexuality was extended by Bishop Mugavero[13] in his ''Pastoral: Human Sexuality'' in 1976 where he states that sexuality is one of God's greatest gifts to man and woman. He supports this idea by the fact that not only does sexuality prepare a person to enter society by assisting in the maturing process, ''but also because it is that aspect of personhood which makes us capable of entering into loving relationships with others.'' The bishop goes on to note that sexuality demands intelligence, honesty and sacrifice that might test our maturity, but he quickly adds that this is no reason to fear sexuality. On the other hand, he urges us to embrace it. However, he thinks that we might fear our own inability to regard it as highly as God who made us sexual persons. He concludes his expressions about the ideal attitude toward sexuality by reminding us that both the married life and the dedicated single life are blessed by God. Jesus indicated the dignity of the married life by elevating it to the level of a sacrament, and he himself endorsed the dedicated single life by his own commitment to celibacy, as he went about doing the Father's will.

Generally, there are two ways of viewing sexuality, especially genital sexuality. One attitude regards sexuality as a drive which must be controlled and consequently a great deal of time and energy is spent on keeping this drive in check. If this is our attitude, we spend a lot of time being very cautious to avoid situations and persons in which the drive could get out of control. This attitude fosters repression of our sexuality. We put chains on our sexuality and are always spending energy being on guard for fear that one of the chains becomes broken and the drive gets out of control.

Another attitude toward sexuality is that it is an aspect of human personality which Almighty God has given us. This attitude approaches sex as one of the many drives of our human nature. If we have this attitude, we use our energy not to repress sexuality but rather to make good decisions with regard to sexuality. As a result, we are aware of our many options and are not restricted to one option, constant repression.

A story illustrates these two attitudes toward sexuality. Two monks were walking alongside the road, and they belonged to an order which viewed all pleasure as sinful or highly suspect. As they were walking, they came to a small lake and wished to cross it. There was a young lady there who was also wanting to cross, but had no means to do this. One monk offered to have the young lady cross the lake on his shoulders as he walked across. She accepted his invitation, and after they reached the other side, he put her down and continued on his journey with his monk friend. A mile later, the second monk broke the long silence and asked why the monk carried that young, attractive lady on his shoulder and placed himself in such a serious temptation. The first monk replied, ''I put the young lady down a mile ago, but you are still carrying her on your shoulders.'' The message behind this story is that the second monk was fantasizing about the young lady for a long period of time and felt very self-righteous that he did not place himself in such a serious temptation as the first. However, the first monk was a man who made a decision among the available options and then forgot about the decision once it was carried out.

Defense Mechanism

When we become anxious or uncomfortable in a certain situation because of our negative attitude toward sexuality, our defense mechanisms come into play to help us reduce these feelings. These defense mechanisms are often processes by which we defend ourselves against unpleasant feelings that tend to expose an unacceptable aspect of ourselves or threaten our self concept. These defenses are unconscious mechanisms that we have learned over the years to assist us in uncomfortable and threatening situations. To achieve this benefit, these defenses demand a certain price on our part because we waste a lot of time and energy as was illustrated in the previous example. The challenge for us is to become aware when we are using them so that we can be more open to our experiences and have more freedom in making decisions about how we are going to live our lives.

Of all the defense mechanisms, *repression* is used more frequently in regards to sexuality than the others. We use it to try to exclude certain experiences from our conscious awareness. We still feel sexual, but refuse to admit to that experience, that is, refuse to acknowledge our own sexuality. In other words, when we use repression, we are living in a world of pretense or false-belief rather than in the real world of which sexuality is a part.

In using repression, we do not choose freely and consciously to use it because that would be a contradiction. Repression is generally an unconscious process. For instance, a woman who constantly represses her sexuality, especially the genital aspect, does not consciously choose to run from this aspect of her personality, but her sexual repression is primarily an automatic process. This type of person seldom allows herself to experience any of her genitality and if her defense mechanism or repression is bluntly pointed out to her, she is likely to feel threatened and to respond to greater defensiveness. Such a person has learned and relearned many times that certain experiences are bad, unacceptable, and a good person would never allow them to take place. Such a person might repress these feelings out of fear, for if she admits them, she risks not only rejection from others, but most importantly, rejection by herself.

Another defense mechanism is *denial* which protects us from unpleasant reality by refusing to face it, often by escapist activities like "getting sick" or being preoccupied with work. An example of denial occurred when a woman wore an extremely suggestive dress which was obvious to others, she refused to believe it even when her co-workers pointed it out to her. Religious sometimes deny their sexuality by becoming "workaholics."

Another defense mechanism frequently used is *rationalization*, a process by which we mentally manipulate facts in order to avoid seeing the obvious. We rationalize when we wish to abstain from seeing the real issue as it is and prefer to justify the way we feel or behave with socially acceptable reasons. Here our sexuality is not denied, but we rationalize sexuality so that we don't face it as it really exists. A priest who was counseling a widow over an extended period of time realized that their relationship was moving towards genital activity. Yet, he rationalized their relationship by stating that it was only pastoral care he was offering and, in addition, that this was being done from the motive of love. However, underneath that rationalization, he feared to admit to himself that their relationship had gone far beyond the bounds of counseling and friendship.

Another defense mechanism important to consider is that of *fantasy* which promotes escaping reality by running off into the world of dreams. A danger of any genital fantasy is that it can isolate a person from the rest of his/her life. The real danger of fantasy is that it offers a person the illusion of intimate fulfillment, responsibility and limits which are all real elements of intimate relations with other people. This type of self-deception robs us of one of the real joys of life, having a close relationship with another human being.

A final defense mechanism is *sublimation* which literally means to lift up or elevate. Sublimation redirects or re-channels one activity which is unacceptable to another which conforms to our value system. If we are using sublimation, we are not only aware of our feelings but decide to use our energy to promote another activity, that is we re-channel that energy.

In both the celibate life and in married life, sublimation at times is used because all genital urgings cannot be acted upon. In married life, a certain control is demanded of a person's genital feelings. One of the most frequently recommended activities to channel the sexual energy is to keep busy in athletics or in manual labor. Oftentimes in high school and in college, there is a strong emphasis on athletic programs to keep the young people occupied so that they could handle their genital feelings. These genital urgings can also be sublimated so that the energy is used in a research project, in attaining a high level of academic achievement, in engaging in some creative activity, in working with the poor or under-privileged children. Since we are human beings, we choose how and where to expend our energy. If I choose to spend many hours becoming extremely proficient in playing the piano, I cannot spend much time practicing my golf swing.[14] So sublimating our sexual energy in appropriate channels can be very beneficial in assisting our general health and very necessary in promoting our Christian value system. In this way it differs from the other defense mechanisms mentioned.

The Myths About Sexuality

In spite of our efforts to attain a positive attitude and to reduce the use of our defense mechanisms concerning sexuality, we live in a world that has many myths, and especially myths concerning genital sexuality. It is difficult not to absorb some of these myths and to begin to assume they are true. Many TV commercials and other advertisements use these myths directly or indirectly, to try to sell their products.

In order to more clearly recognize these myths, it is profitable for us to indicate some of them. The first and possibly most dangerous myth is that man and woman have been destined by God to live forever in complete happiness. This is an impossibility; no human being including Jesus Christ has ever been happy all of his/her life. It is impossible to live a life where everything goes right all the time, and maybe it is impossible to live one week where everything goes according to our wishes. Another aspect of this myth is that we can live in an anxiety-free life. There are bound to be certain situations that occur frequently in our lives that make us more or less anxious. To support this myth, some of us have the idea that "If I get my Ph.D., or marry this or that person, or take this vacation, or move into this part of town, or buy this automobile, I will be happy." From experience, all of us know that the things we long to attain make us happy and content only for a time, but not forever.

The second myth is that genital sex is a crucial part of being a human person; it's so special that when sex is had, lights will flash, bells will ring and the persons will be in a state of ecstasy. When people have sexual intercourse with these exceedingly high expectations, they generally are severely disappointed. One young man who began having sexual relationships in high school said that he had these expectations and now concludes, "Sex is not such a big deal after all." Now, eight years later, the same man states that, "Like the rest of life, sex is what you make it. It's not a magical force with its own power to save you, or fulfill you, or whatever. But it took me a long time to sort that out and to stop blaming myself as a failure."

Another myth akin to that one, is that genital sex makes people happy. If we are sad, if things aren't going right in our life, then our cultural myth tells us that sex will cure our ills. In reality, there is no one cure for everyone's ills. Sometimes it even happens that people who are sad, become unhappier through genital sex because they feel more lonely than before, because they now feel guilty, and because they feel used.

Genital sex means instant intimacy is the fourth myth. Another way of phrasing this is to understand that celibacy means the absence of intimacy. The physical intimacy of sexual relations doesn't guarantee "real intimacy," which is sharing on a deep level with another person. It means sharing feelings, opinions, significant happenings and goals with one another. A celibate person can share in depth or be intimate with several people while a married person is not necessarily intimate even with one person.

The fifth myth is extremely common in our American culture — marriage relieves loneliness. If people are lonely before marriage, they are likely to be lonely after marriage. If a person is extremely lonely, it often means that the person has difficulty in interpersonal relationships, and marriage does not solve that, but rather focuses on that problem in a person's life. Physical closeness does not mean loneliness is resolved. How often is it not stated that people have been lonely in a crowd which means that they have not established any close relationships with anyone in that crowd. Besides, loneliness is better tolerated by those who live alone; they have no expectations about marriage solving their pain of loneliness and so have no disappointments. Lonely people who marry have about the same chance of realizing their expectations as the host at a party who insists that everybody have a good time.[15]

The sixth myth is that celibacy is a life of sacrifice. Celibacy means a life of sacrificing genital sexual pleasure, but there are many other pleasures available to the celibate person, namely, a certain independence, and the ability to serve the Lord in a particular way that one chooses. Another myth is that celibacy and sexuality mean the same thing to everyone. Certainly celibacy and sexuality mean one thing to one religious woman and to another religious woman in the same congregation, it means something else. Because of our cultural heritage, celibacy and sexuality often differ for religious women and religious men. Another aspect is that what celibacy and sexuality meant ten years ago to a religious person, it does not mean today. Many religious men and women in their formation days, were given the concepts of sexuality and celibacy that their founder or foundress had, or the concepts their spiritual director held. As these religious people matured and digested these concepts, no doubt they changed drastically. These differences in concepts of sexuality and celibacy are healthy because there are many different aspects to them.[16]

Affective Sexuality—Intimacy

I would like to continue discussing myths by again rejecting the myth that sexuality is co-extensive with genitality. Sexuality enables us to enter other person's lives as friends and to encourage them to enter our lives. It makes us dependent on others, allows others to depend on us, and gets us involved with them. It is a relational power which allows us to be open-to-others, sensitive, understanding, warm, gentle, compassionate and mutually supportive. Thus it enables us to be intimate with others, to be affectively sexual.

When we have formed intimate relationships, our lives become full and enjoyable and not just an existence. The challenge we have is to transform our lives to make them truly meaningful, to escape the slavery of the ignorance of how to love. In other words, our challenge is to know how to use our sexuality for giving life, for truly loving, for deep and lasting relationships.[17] However, to do this, we must trust others and not be fearful of becoming dependent upon them. Psychologists state that it is a well known fact that some people have a strong revulsion to sexuality because of their will to be totally independent. So sexuality is that relational aspect of our personality that reminds us of our need for others, of our dependence upon them.[18]

Associated with our fear of dependency on another, is our fear of being swallowed up by them. Many times in marriage or in a close friendship, we will only go so far for fear that if we go further, we will be swallowed up by the other person. Sometimes in marriage, a spouse will mention that she/he is willing to meet half of the other person's needs, but will go no further because the other person constantly will develop new needs, and as a result, the individual will lose his/her identity. This is one of the fears of relating on a close level with another person or one of the fears of intimacy. One reason we fear losing our own identity is that our identity is unclear and is built on sand. If we are solid in our identity, then this fear would decrease.

A beautiful example of the intimacy about which we are talking occurs in the Book of Jonah. There, Jonah is swallowed up by the whale and becomes, as it were, one with the whale, living in the belly of the whale. Once he is vomited up by the whale on the shore of Niniveh, he becomes a new person. Before this he was a resistant, fearful person who rejects God's command. Once he experiences intimacy, he is a new individual. Now he is a God—centered, spirit—filled, determined and open person. Intimacy enabled Jonah to become a new person.

In order to understand who we are, that is, to attain a clear identity about ourselves, it is important for us to become intimate like Jonah did. Intimacy is a need that all of us have in order to become new individuals. This ties in with Jesus' words that unless we lose our lives, we will not be able to have life. In other words, unless we lose ourselves in someone else, as Jonah did in the belly of the whale, we cannot really be our own true person. For by sharing ourselves with another, we come to a greater understanding of who we are as persons. At the same time, there is fear and hope involved. There is fear of being swallowed up by another, the fear of not being able to be free to make decisions for ourselves any more, and there is hope present too, the hope that through intimacy we can grow. Our challenge is to overcome our fear in order to allow ourselves to grow.[19]

Intimacy, is being known and knowing the other person. In this experience of being known by another and being accepted by another for who we are, we begin to believe in ourselves, to believe that it is wonderful that we exist. In this process, we ever so slowly come to believe that certain aspects of our personality or of our bodily image which we find unacceptable, which embarrasses us, can in fact be accepted by some human being. This acceptance enables us to learn to own and love every aspect of our beings, that is, to own and love our history with its many wonderful feelings and even to own our sinfulness. We no longer have a need to be perfect to be lovable. When we have been deeply affirmed by someone who really loves us, and once we accept that affirmation, then we are on the road to allowing God to love us, precisely because he knows us with our strengths and weaknesses. Thus there is harmony between growth in human and divine intimacy.[20]

As a result of the other person's acceptance and understanding, we have a true friend. We have someone upon whom we can depend, someone whom we need not fear, someone with whom we can be vulnerable, someone with whom we can be dependent without being destroyed. At the same time, our friend is someone who can be dependent upon us, and whose dependency needs we choose to meet. In other words, there is a healthy degree of mutual dependence in intimacy of one friend upon another or one spouse upon another. This demands a great degree of work since it is no easy task.[21]

When we have attained a deep friendship with another person, we will still experience periodic moments of loneliness because this is part of being a human being. However, our loneliness will not exist for a prolonged period because it results from a lack of contact or linkage with our world. People who are continually lonely do so because they fail to feel in some way that they are having an impact on another, that being alive makes some difference for some person in the world. Since they lack this sense of meaning or impact, they experience loneliness. Another aspect of this need for contact or linkage is that lonely people do not possess a meaningful relationship with another. We who have deep relationships with others, experience this contact. For us, we have meaning or purpose in life. We have the rich blessing of a meaningful relationship with another. Thus, loneliness will not be a frequent part of our lives.[22]

The degree of intimacy or affective sexuality depends primarily on our relationships and motivations. This may involve marital love, a close friendship, a gracious meeting or a warm recognition. Affective sexual behavior can be an end in itself or it can be a means of attaining genital behavior. A warm smile or a gentle embrace (affective sexual behavior) can be ends in themselves, or they may simply be the steps that lead to sexual intercou.se. Confusion results when all expressions of affection or intimacy are classified as preludes to genital behavior.

The intentions of the people exchanging signs of affection are extremely important in determining whether the affective sexuality is an end in itself or a means leading to genital activity. A difficulty arises when there is a conflict concerning the intentions. A woman may show signs of affection for a man with no intention of this leading to genitality, but her friend may misinterpret her intention and consequently feel that she is encouraging genital intimacy. On the other hand, a man may have only the intention of showing simple affections to his close friend but become genitally aroused. Here there is conflict between his intention and his feeling.

Examples of Intimate Friendships

Having spoken of the value of intimacy, it is important to see how intimate friendships were viewed in the life of the Church. Aelred of Rievaulx, a twelfth century Cistercian monk, gives us a beautiful treatise on the subject of friendship. Aelred's discussion is valuable because he is not speaking solely from theory, but his ideas arise out of his own experience in life. His own friendship with Waldef and Walter Daniel are well known. Aelred viewed friendship as a creation of human effort and a gift of God. He discusses friendship among celibate people in his letter entitled, ''Spiritual Friendship'' where he states:

> ''There is no more powerful, more efficacious, more excellent remedy for our wounds, in everything that comes to pass in this life, than the possession of someone who comes to console us and sympathize with us when we suffer disappointments and comes running to congratulate us when we have met with success. ''Two friends,'' says the Apostle Paul, ''help carry one another's burden; in fact, each finds his own burden smaller than that of the other. Friendship, then, adds light to happiness and alleviates misfortune because it sympathetically shares burdens. Indeed, in this life, a friend is the best remedy of all.''[23]

In the seventeenth century, Francis De Sales gives us a much more cautious view of intimate friendships in his book, *Introduction To the Devout Life*. In order to understand the reason for these different approaches, it is important to note that Francis De Sales lived in an entirely different era than Aelred of Rievaulx. Francis lived at a time when intimate friendships were frequently leading to genital activity. So he spoke about the dangers of friendships rather than of their great benefit. This cautiousness about intimate friendships influenced the spirituality of the Church until the twentieth century. Most older religious and priests were trained to be very careful during their formation days about forming particular friendships. In spite of this, there are many examples in the Church's history of intimate friendships that existed among people of the same sex as well as people of different sexes. Aelred of Rievaulx speaks of the benefits of close friendship among the monks while Jordan of Saxony in the twelfth century speaks of the glories of heterosexual relationships. In his letters, he expresses his affection to Diane d'Andalo, a Dominican nun, and specifically shares the pain of absence and separation from her in these words:

> "Yet I cannot wonder that you are sad, when I am far from you since do what I may, I myself cannot but be sad that you are so far from me."
> "When I have to part from you, I do so with heavy heart; yet you add sorrow to my sorrow since I see you then so inconsolably weighed down that I cannot but be saddened, not only by our separation which afflicts us both, but also by your own desolation as well."[24]

In addition to his close relationship to Diane, he had an intimate friendship with Henry of Cologne who entered the Dominican Order with him. So here we have an example of a man who had friendships on the heterosexual level as well as with people of his own sex.

There are other examples of extremely close relationships in history. Possibly the most well known is that between Clare and Francis of Assisi. Clare was only eighteen years old when she met Francis and left her home and family to follow him. Although they lived separately, they remained in constant communication with one another. During a visit with Clare at San Damiano, Francis wrote his famous "Canticle of Brother Sun."

Another couple that is famous for their intimate friendship is Theresa of Avila and John of the Cross. Both of these celibates were quite ardent and sensual in their writings to each other. They lived close together for six years at the convent in Avila while Theresa served as Prioress and John as Spiritual Director and Confessor. During this time, Theresa wrote her passionate *Interior Castle* and John began his famous, amorous *Spiritual Canticle*. It is interesting to note that even though Theresa was 27 years older than John, this did not seem to deter their love. On the contrary, their love for each other seemed to help them attain the spiritual heights in intimacy in prayer about which they wrote.[25]

There are many other examples of intimate friendships in our Church's history. Famous friendships between men are: Jesus and John, Basil and Gregory Nazianyen, Bernard of Clairvaux and William of Thierry, Aelred and Waldef, Jordan of Saxony and Henry of Cologne. There are a number of equally famous friendships between men and women: Catherine of Siena and Raymond of Capua, Francis De Sales and Jane Frances Chantal, Vincent de Paul and Louise De Marillac, and Teilhard de Chardin and Leontine Zanta.[26]

Such intimate friendships always have their dangers but, at the same time, they are a source of strength, beauty, growth and ability to love Almighty God. It is simply impossible to love everyone in general when we cannot love anyone in particular.

The Integration of Sexuality

Often when the word "integration" is used, it means that we take something that we know intellectually and move that to what we experience in the gut level. For example, on a theoretical level or the intellectual level, we know that it is better to express our anger to another, but on the gut level it takes some time to feel comfortable in sharing our upsetness, irritation or anger with another person. When we speak here about the integration of sexuality, we are speaking about this aspect of integration in the sense that we are urging a positive outlook toward sexuality to enable us to feel comfortable with our own and other's sexuality.

Integration in this context also means that we realize that integration means "whole." There is a tendency in our culture to look upon sexuality in a fragmented way—we only look upon the genital aspects of another person rather than consider the whole person who has genital components. For instance, a man might be sexually attracted to a woman and realize that she is well-formed and has beautiful breasts. However, there are no such things as breasts and well proportioned hips in the abstract, but only as components of a woman who has many other aspects to her personhood. What kind of person is she socially, intellectually, psychologically, and spiritually? If we only look at her from the genital attractiveness, we are fragmenting her, instead of looking at the whole person, we are seeing her purely as a sex symbol, seeing her purely as a physical person rather than understanding her personality, etc.

In order to see persons in their wholeness, it's important for us to look again. We see them originally by what attracts us, which possibly is their physical being. If we take a second look, we see very clearly that attractiveness and other aspects of the whole person. Sometimes nurses make comments about a male patient, speaking about how broad a chest the young man has, how nicely formed the hair is on his chest and that it's not too much hair so as to look like a bear, but just a sufficient amount to make him sexually attractive to them. When they talk about him only in this light, they are looking at him from a very narrow viewpoint, instead of seeing him as a total person with a spiritual, intellectual, social and psychological dimension.

Speaking of integration, we don't want to confine it to the total person either. We choose also to look at the *total relationship*. Sometimes one might not only isolate a physical aspect of an individual, e.g., a woman's breasts or a man's hairy chest, but also one individual act and not evaluate that act as part of a total relationship. In fantasy, one might imagine having genital intercourse with a person who is not his/her spouse and daydream how pleasurable that will be. Integrating one's sexuality, she/he would realize that this act is not going to end with a walk off in the sunset with his/her partner, living happily ever after. This genital act cannot simply be totally forgotten. And what about the future of this relationship with the other person? Is there any possibility of marriage, and if there is, can this marriage be a happy union in which there is much more involved than just genital activity? Are we in any way compatible psychologically, intellectually, emotionally, spiritually? We have a tendency to isolate acts and to buy into the movie theme that we're simply going to live happily ever after without realizing all the ramifications of an individual act. As mature individuals, we look upon sexuality as being part of the total person and upon genital activity as being part of a total relationship with another individual rather than as the whole relationship with another person.

Integration means that we not only have a positive attitude toward all aspects of sexuality, but also that we view other people as whole persons instead of viewing simply fragmented sexual parts of them. It means that we realize that genital activity has many implications attached to it including its psychological and spiritual aspects. Often in experiencing genital urgings, one experiences a desire not so much for genital intimacy as we are for psychological and spiritual intimacy with another individual. So, it is profitable to investigate the genital feelings and to understand what they really mean.

Psychosexual Maturity and Immaturity

When pastoral care persons have integrated their sexuality into their total personhood, they can look beyond the physical attractiveness of an individual and see the total person. This does not mean that they deny the physical attractiveness of the other, but they see more than that. It means that in expressing their sexuality, they are not limited to the genital, but can relate to others in many different ways. They acknowledge the sexual attraction between themselves and others without allowing such an attraction to become compulsively genital. They admit that they experience their own sexuality and the sexuality of others, and at the same time, seek deep relationships with other people. In their ministry, these pastoral people touch another as an expression of warmth and concern without having any covert intention of arousing genital activity in themselves and others.

The psychosexually mature person easily admits loving other individuals and does not attempt to make that love abstract by saying that they love humanity. Nor do these persons attempt to spiritualize that human love by saying simply that they are just following the command of Christ to love everyone. Such persons, because of their maturity, admit that they are attracted to another person, and have a deep relationship with him/her to the point that they can say that they love the other person. In this deep relationship, mature pastoral persons are able to be intimate without dominating the other individual, without attempting to possess them, to control or manipulate them, without being jealous of their time and their association with others. They are aware when problems arise that are within themselves or within their relationships, and seek appropriate assistance.

It seems that the more mature the pastoral persons are, the more unity that will exist between their espoused values and their private thoughts and behaviors. These individuals prize their values highly and treat them with respect. Their values are not based solely on authority and so they don't respond simply out of obedience. Their values can stand on their own apart from any authority, and such persons are open to the guidance of persons in authority. Their values are in process too, that is, alive and active, not static. Thus, they commit themselves to certain values, know how to cope with conflicts in their lives, and assume responsibility for the consequences of their choices. If they violate a certain value, they do not immediately blame someone else or instincts of nature.

In visiting the sick, mature pastoral persons are aware when they feel attracted to a certain person, or when a patient or a relative of a patient is attracted to them. One woman chaplain was visiting a dying cancer patient and the husband was usually present. During the first few visits, the husband told her of his difficulties managing at home without his wife, his loneliness, etc. He invited her to come to his home at night so that she might cook supper for him and perform some household chores. Immediately, she perceived all this was a cover-up for his interest in her as a sexual person and not in her pastoral ministry. Because of her awareness of his covert expressions of genitality, she told him, "No," and further made it very clear that she was a ministerial person whose ministry was limited to the hospital setting. At the same time, she did not run away from this man, but continued to visit him and his wife. A seminarian chaplain was asked by a female patient, "Tuck me in and kiss me goodnight." An immature chaplain would have run away from that situation in his anxiety, but this chaplain sat down with her and initiated a conversation about how much she wanted to be married and how lonely she was as a single person.

Fr. Donald Goergen thinks that these are the signs of psychosexual maturity: 1) the capacity to love myself; 2) the capacity to love persons of the other sex; 3) the capacity to love persons of my own sex; 4) the capacity to love God; 5) the capacity to love in a nonpossessive way; 6) the capacity to love physically; 7) the capacity to communicate tender and warm feelings; 8) the capacity for genital love and orgasm; 9) the capacity to distinguish sexual desire and sexual love; 10) the capacity to integrate sexual desire into a loving relationship.[28]

Psychosexually immature pastoral persons compensate extensively in thought, affect and behavior. One form of compensation occurs when pastoral persons participate vicariously in the heterosexual activities of their parishioners or patients. They encourage people to speak often or in great detail about their genital activities and compensate in this way for their lack of genital expression. Another form of compensation happens when pastoral persons take a great deal of interest in the struggles that celibates have in remaining celibate. When persons revolve the conversation around sexual matters constantly, it usually is a sign of their immaturity.

Another form of compensation is to deny or demean the value and pleasure of genital expression. Celibates are tempted to deny the legitimate value of sexual expression or to make fun of it, and in this way, indicate their lack of psychosexual maturity. Others compensate by taking refuge in sexual fantasies which offer them gratification and conquests. This is simply substitution. When pastoral care people are celibate and frequently use compensatory measures, they are struggling intensely with the challenges of celibacy and their ministry is hampered as a result.

When priests, sisters and seminarians regard celibacy as an excessive burden and feel that the Church is depriving them of a legitimate avenue of communication by imposing celibacy, their pastoral effectiveness is limited. This feeling of being "cheated" because of the Church's law, expresses itself as these people minister in their various settings, e.g., "poor me." These people are psychosexually immature and need to work through these feelings of anger at the authorities of the Church and of being unjustly deprived of genital expression. Such persons experience severe internal conflicts and their immaturity influences their behavior to the extent that they frequently seek gratifications covertly.[29]

Sometimes immature pastoral care persons express their immaturity by denying their sexuality and the sexuality of the persons to whom they are ministering, and other times by simply being naive. One woman student chaplain visited a 65 year old widower who frequently bragged about his three different girl friends visiting him during his hospitalization. He urged her to visit him daily saying, "Come every day. You make me feel better." This student presented her conversation with him as a verbatim to her peers for feedback. When one of them asked if she felt he was flirting with her, she was surprised that any student would bring this up. She denied that he would have any motive like that and felt that he just enjoyed her ministry but did not relate to her as a sexual person.

Another example of immaturity occurred in my own life as a student supervisor. I appeared before a committee requesting a feedback on how I had supervised my five students. One of the committee persons asked me how I felt about this particular woman student I had. I answered him in a very vague way and said that I had no particular feelings about her, even though he knew that she was an attractive woman. He began pushing me, "Did she turn you on? Was she sexy? What kind of legs did she have?" These questions embarrassed me and I was unable to respond. This was because I was too immature to admit that I was a sexual being and found this woman student attractive.

Another example of how a person's immaturity affected his ministry occurred with a student chaplain. Initially, he came to the program dressed in a shirt and tie, but then during the third week of the program discarded that attire and began coming to the program with an open shirt so that his hairy chest was showing. When people commented about his sporty or sexy attire, he denied this and claimed that it was just too hot to wear a shirt and tie. It was difficult to accept this denial because the room where we had our classes and the hospital where he visited patients were air-conditioned. This student was expressing his psychosexual immaturity by seeking their affirmation of him as a sexual man.

It is not certain that one or the other action or affect of a person indicates that she/he is psychosexually immature. But there are some general indicators of a person's maturity or immaturity. However, from her experience as a religious woman and a psychologist, Sr. Susanne Breckel thinks that these are signs of a person's psychosexual immaturity: 1) awkward around people of the opposite sex, e.g., don't know where to put feet or what to say; 2) must be around "the boys or girls" all the time and is uncomfortable being alone; 3) hides behind his or her role and is never seen as a real person; 4) relates as a "thing" to others rather than as a man or a woman; 5) relates to people as a super-intellectual and only relates to others from the head up. She goes on to say that sometimes this immaturity is displayed through chemical dependency on drugs or alcohol and other times it's expressed through an excessive interest in sports or a person's work. She concludes any excessive interest in a particular area, is a possible sign of a person's immaturity.[30]

In conclusion, pastoral care persons need to be aware of their sexuality in order to minister effectively. Pastoral persons are constantly relating to people, not through their role, but as human beings who have a sexual dimension. It is important that pastoral persons be comfortable with their own sexuality as well as with others' sexuality. It is important that they have integrated their sexuality into their total person so that they do not deny their sexuality or forget that there are other aspects to an individual's personality besides the sexual.

Footnotes

1. Gn 1:28.
2. Gn 2:18.
3. Gn 2:23.
4. Sg 1:2B-4D.
5. Sg 4:3-6.
6. Sg 5:10B-15.
7. Donald Goergen, *The Sexual Celibate* (New York: Seabury Press, 1974), pp. 14-25.
8. Theodore W. Jennings, "Theological Perspectives on Sexuality," *The Journal of Pastoral Care*, March, 1979, p. 4.
9. Paul Marx, "The Meaning of Human Sexuality," *Audio Theology Digest*, (Canfield, OH: Alba House Communications, 1975).
10. Wm. F. Kraft, *Sexual Dimensions of the Celibate Life*, (Kansas City: Andrews and McMeel, Inc., 1979), pp. 36-40.
11. Donald Goergen, *op. cit.*, pp. 16-36.
12. Wm. C. McFadden, "Sexuality and the Church," *America*, Oct. 21, 1978, pp. 262-5.
13. Bishop Francis J. Mugavero, "Pastoral: Human Sexuality," *National Catholic Reporter*, March 5, 1979, p. 8.
14. Wm. F. Kraft, *op. cit.*, pp. 66-82.
15. Wm. J. Lederer and Dr. Don D. Jackson, *The Mirages of Marriage*, (New York: W.W. Norton & Co., 1968), pp. 75-8.
16. John J. Malecki and Susanne Breckel, "Sexuality: The Celibate Response," *National Assembly of Religious Brothers*, (Passionsist Broadcasting, West Springfield, MA, 1978), tape 1.
17. Bishop Francis J. Mugavero, *op. cit.*, p. 8.
18. Theodore W. Jennings, *op. cit.*, p. 5.
19. David Back, "Bring A Person Into Being," *A Christian Approach*, (Marina Del-Rey, CA: Creative Audio-Visual Co., 1977).
20. Bernard J. Bush, "I Have Called You By Name," *Intimacy*, Anna Polcino, ed. (Whitinsville, MA: Affirmation Books, 1978), p. 48.

21. Donald Goergen, *op. cit.,* p. 150.
22. Richard J. Gilmartin, "Loneliness and Narcissism," *Loneliness,* James P. Madden, Ed., (Whitinsville, MA: Affirmation Books, 1977), p. 79.
23. Aelred of Rievaulx, "Spiritual Friendship," 2nd French Translation in THE LIBRARY OF MEDIEVAL SPIRITUALITY (Brussels, 1948), pp. 53-57; and "The Friendless Man Is Truly Alone," *Christian Readings,* Vol. 4, Year 1, (New York: Catholic Book Publishing Co.), p. 71.
24. "To Heaven With Diana," letter 35. Also Donald Goergen, *op. cit.,* p. 171.
25. Janis Gustafson, *Celibate Passion* (Scranton, PA: Harper & Row Inc. 1978), pp. 100-101.
26. Rubert Murry, "Spiritual Friendship," *The Way,* Supplement 10, 1970, pp. 61-73.
27. Wm. F. Kraft, *op. cit.,* pp. 85-93.
28. Donald Goergen, *op. cit.,* pp. 178-9.
29. Philip D. Cristantiello, Psychosexual Maturity in Celibate Development" *Review for Religious,* Sept. 1978, pp. 652-4.
30. John J. Malecki and Susanne Breckel, *op. cit.,* tape 1.

CHAPTER EIGHT

GROUPS

Today we form groups and have meetings about almost everything. Pastoral persons need to be aware of the dynamics that are taking place in meetings and how to intervene effectively to assist the members in attaining their goal. Knowledge of group dynamics was important to me in a recent meeting which I had with the personnel of the labor and delivery department to discuss our practice of baptizing newborn infants at the hospital.

The meeting for the night and day shifts began at 6:30 A.M. with the head nurse introducing me to the group. I explained to the Catholic and Protestant nurses that the Catholic Church has undergone some changes since the Second Vatican Council and one of the changes concerned the sacrament of Baptism. Formerly, the church urged us to baptize every dying infant, no matter what the parent's religion, because the baby has a right to heaven which could only be attained through baptism. Now, as a result of new insights, the church suggests that we baptize only those babies whose parents wish it and that we offer a prayer over a stillborn infant, rather than baptize a dead person.

After my explanation of the change in policy regarding baptism, I asked for comments or questions. Initially there was a period of silence which was broken by Maureen, the head nurse, who asked if there were some nurses who might want to comment on this change. One nurse, Pam, spoke up with this encouragement and firmly denounced such radical ideas, claiming that they were completely contradictory to what she was taught as a student in nursing school. The more she spoke, the angrier she became. When she stopped, Sandy chimed in that the

Catholic Church has changed enough, and she didn't want any more changes. Connie followed by stating that there was nothing wrong with their present policy, and she didn't intend to change in spite of what I said.

At this point I asked the value of giving sacraments to a dead person and how they would feel if a minister performed a religious ceremony for their child without their knowledge or against their wishes.

Several other nurses responded that prayers are valuable at any time by anyone, and went on to comment how much damage this new teaching would have on Catholic patients, who would not agree with this radical practice. No one even hinted that this new policy might have any good aspects to it while several seemed relieved to know it was not sinful if they continued their practice of baptizing all critically ill babies.

This is an example of one group interaction, and what happened in that group happens in many groups. It's beneficial for those who lead groups to understand group dynamics; it's beneficial for persons who participate in many groups (parish council, worship committee, finance committee, education committee, etc.), to know about group dynamics like the one just mentioned.

Benefits of a Group Decision

One of the shortcomings of the past in the Church's life has been the fact that bishops and pastors made decisions all by themselves. In so doing they never benefited from the skill the lay persons could have brought to the situation. Today this has been remedied by establishing pastoral councils, building committees and many others. Ideally in these groups input is obtained from various people with different backgrounds and so the group benefits from many experiences and skills of a variety of people. It is true that "many heads are better than one," but it is not beneficial just to emphasize pure numbers on a committee without any emphasis on qualified people to assist in searching for the best decisions.

When a person functions autonomously, he can become narrow minded and easily get into a rut. In the group process new blood is brought to the situation and assists in attaining a fresh look at the problem. In the Professional Advisory Committee which assisted me in performing a self-study of the Clinical Pastoral Education Program at the hospital, persons from the following departments were members: administration, social service, nursing service, staff education and field education from a local seminary. These persons brought different backgrounds to the committee and were excellent in preparing for the site visit by an accreditation team of Clinical Pastoral Education. Their variety of backgrounds offered far more help than if the committee were composed entirely of clergy persons.

Another benefit in shared decision-making is that it assists people in accepting the decisions. Persons want to become meaningfully involved in solving their own problems and in making decisions that affect them. When persons do not participate, they tend to react; they attack, complain, and look for a scapegoat. On the other hand, when persons help share the events and decisions which influence their lives, they more readily accept those decisions. When a bishop made a decision and then made it known to the priests and laity of the diocese through regular chancery letters and the diocesan weekly newspaper, the response was often indifference or severe, angry criticism. At this point too, the bishop had to sell his plan to the priests and laity. He had to spend time explaining his reasons for choosing his particular plan, and the means he chose to attain his goal. Later, if the bishop's plan was not successful, it was easy for everyone to blame the bishop for the failure instead of taking some responsibility themselves. Presently, if the pastoral council is not working effectively, the priests and laity are less apt to blame the persons they elected to that council, and more likely to put forth a great deal of effort to make the project succeed.

Finally, group participation assists persons in understanding the decision and the means necessary to implement it. They know the other alternatives that were rejected because they seemed to have less advantages. So they are more convinced that this choice is the best one and are more motivated to see that goal is achieved.

When the liturgy changes came after the Second Vatican Council, the priests were not involved in making any of these changes and often did not understand the reasons behind them. They simply were told to carry them out. Frequently priests unfortunately modeled that approach with their parishioners and just announced that Mass would be in English, the altar would be turned around, guitars would replace the organ, and congregational singing would replace silence, and sometimes even the church choir. Neither the priests nor the people were adequately prepared for these changes and as a result, both often felt forced to implement something they did not understand or accept. Naturally, this did not enable them to receive the changes with an open mind.[1]

Essentials to Group Effectiveness

Two essential elements for the effectiveness of any group are listening and communicating. Each person has the obligation to listen to what the others are saying and to ask questions to clarify the messaage. Naturally, if we are simply waiting until the other person stops talking so that a rebuttal can be given, there is little listening. We cannot truly listen if we are formulating our response to the other person's statement. The characteristic required is openness to the ideas and feelings of the persons in the group. A closed person is not really capable of listening. In the sample interaction with the nurses in labor and delivery, I question how much listening took place and how open the nurses were to the new ideas because of the many years this policy has been in practice and because of their identification with mothers whose infants were critically ill or had died.

Associated with listening is the ability to communicate clearly. Sometimes we fail to communicate clearly because we have not thought thoroughly through our ideas ourselves. We thereby express them in a confusing manner. Other times we fail because we are not in touch with our own feelings, so naturally cannot share them. Another reason for our lack of communicating effectively is fear that our ideas and feelings will not be accepted. As a result, in expressing them we are very anxious and possibly skip some aspect of our message which prevents true communication. Trust needs to be established before much sharing can occur.

The final essential element is cooperation, instead of competition. When a group is cooperating, their behavior is directed toward common goals rather than each person striving toward his/her own goal at the expense of other members. Often in the initial stages of negotiation between union and management, much competition rather than cooperation, is experienced. Each side appears competitive, striving to acheive its goals at the expense of the other.

When competition prevails in a group, threats and bluffs are used instead of genuine concern for seeking the best solution to a problem. Logical as well as irrational arguments are used rather than logical and innovative arguments. Misrepresentation of one's own needs and not allowing others to know exactly what is wanted and how much one is willing to give up to obtain it are present, instead of an open and honest representation to one's needs. During this period of competition, individuals or factions of the group make themselves appear better than others. There is an emphasis on superiority versus inferiority, and emphasis on "we vs. they." There is also a tendency to distort perceptions of others; people perceive they understand the other person's proposal, but in reality they don't. In this atmosphere there is a distortion of judgments; we tend to evaluate one's contributions as the best and to downgrade the others. In general, competitive members are so eager to attain their goals that they stereotype other persons, ignore their logic and increase the level of hostility. On the other hand, in an atmosphere of cooperation attention is given to others, communication and understanding prevail, and group support is present rather than individual defensive reactions. The members who have the spirit of cooperation are determined to drop stereotypes, give ideas consideration on the basis of their own merit regardless of their source, and attempt to eliminate hostility.

Competition is important in many aspects of our lives, e.g., in business, sports, etc. However, in a group where the members are supposed to be working together to attain a common goal, cooperation is essential because the members need to utilize all their abilities to reach their common goal.

Qualities of Leadership

One style of leadership all of us have been familiar with are authoritarian leaders. They leave no doubt who is boss. They might be termed the "ram-rod" decision-makers. They trust only their insights and think that a group is a waste of time. Their idea of a successful meeting is one in which they manipulate the group to agree with their ideas by open or subtle use of power. These persons are insecure and so keep as much pertinent information and influence to themselves. They understand only one type of meeting, a win-lose situation, and of course, they always want to win. They abhor indecisiveness because it appears to them as weakness. They detest committees because they seem slow and inefficient.

A second type of leadership are the "contented-cow" decision-makers. These are the persons whose highest value is agreement. Peace at any price is the motto of these leaders who fear conflict, thinking that it results only in hurt feelings and alienation. They presume that no good will ever come from conflict. These persons function on the analogous premise that the contented cow produces more milk. They operate on the principle that it's more important to keep harmony in the group than to come up with the best possible solution. Thus in the group the task is cooperation and avoidance of conflict. Such persons are "nice guys" who are always pleasant and smiling, but nobody knows what they really think because they avoid sharing personal opinions. It's hard to get angry at such persons because they are so nice, yet it's easy to become enraged at them because the members of the committee are dealing with a thing, a non-person rather than an individual who has feelings and ideas.

The third style of leadership are the "cop-outs." These persons don't believe in groups, nor in shared decision-making. They prefer to make decisions alone, but since that is impossible, they tolerate groups. They also abhor disagreement and shun conflict at all costs. As a result, they sit on the sidelines, hoping the meeting will soon be over and that somehow everyone will leave the meeting happy and on friendly terms. These individuals don't make any contributions normally, but if a conflict arises they might suggest that an outside arbitrator be brought in to restore peace to the group.

The "tongue-in-cheek" decision-makers are the fourth style. These persons want their way, but realize that shared decision-making is the "in thing" to do and so they go along with it. They seem willing to confer, to share with others, to modify their positions to reflect other persons' viewpoints, but these things are done to gain agreement with "tongue-in-cheek," not because they believe the modifications are an improvement on their original proposal. Their goal before a meeting is to figure out how much they must give up to have the majority approve of their ideas. They are closed to new insights, and are interested in only getting their ideas accepted by the majority. Since there is a great emphasis on "the majority rules," these persons appear very democratic and seem to follow the American way of life.

The final style of leadership in groups are the "creative" leaders. These persons sincerely believe in the value of groups and want to have the assistance of others in making a decision. They are secure in themselves and realize they don't have all the answers, so they are anxious to have input from others. These persons are aware of their own giftedness and of their limitations, so they seek to improve decisions by having the assistance of others who have knowledge and abilities which they don't possess. They also know that sometimes in the group process, conflicts occur, but they view conflict as the breeding-ground for new ideas. These persons believe in the creative potential of the members of any group rather than fearing others or seeking to pacify others who might disagree with one another.[2] Thus, the qualifications of effective leaders are persons who are caring, emotional, stimulating, offer meaningful contributions and perform the executive functions well. Caring leaders offer support, praise their members, accept others and different viewpoints, possess warmth and protect those persons who might be injured excessively in the group process. The emotionally stimulating leaders are those who are challenging, appropriately confrontive, and share their own opinions and feelings. Those leaders offer meaningful contributions who explain, clarify, interpret, and translate feelings and experiences into meaningful ideas. The leaders who perform the executive functions well are those who set limits, have rules and goals, manage time well, intercede effectively and suggest procedures appropriately.[3]

Individual Group Members

In every group different personalities influence people to act differently. Some of different kinds of people present in groups are: the aggressor, the peace-maker, the clarifier, the blocker, the evaluator, the giver of information, the giver of advice, the information seeker. It's profitable to reflect on the initial example of group interaction to see the various roles of the different members. In the sample group, the head nurse functioned as the structurer by introducing me as the speaker for the meeting, calling the meeting to order, coming with an agenda for the meeting, and appointing a person to take the minutes. She also functioned as the initiator by inviting her personnel to voice their opinions when there was silence. The secretary for the meeting adopted the role of a clarifier so that she could accurately take minutes. The first nurses who spoke in the meeting adopted the role of aggressors with their emotional responses. I saw myself function as reflector by asking the nurses if it made sense to continue their practice of baptizing babies who were already dead, and how they would feel if some minister of a different religion performed a religious ceremony over their child without their consent. At the end of the meeting I felt like a peace-maker when I shook hands with the nurses who strongly opposed any change of policy. Interestingly in this group interaction no one attempted to be the ''supporter,'' pointing out one good feature to the suggested policy, and a number sat in silence playing the role of observer. Another noteworthy fact of that experience is that the head nurse did not assume the role of the expeditor to move on to another point on her agenda, but allowed the discussion to continue because it was so emotionally charged.

We can all remember meetings where someone dominated. In the pre-Vatican II era the pastor generally dominated the meetings and if someone voiced an opinion he did not like, he became a ''blocker.'' I know of one pastor who blocked a suggestion he opposed by telling the people simply that he would retire from the parish if they insisted on their idea. No doubt we have been at other meetings where there were ''recognition seekers'' who always wanted it known how much and how many years they have worked for the parish. Finally, every committee seems to have a ''distractor'' who goes off on a tangent giving a lengthy, dull explanation of something the people know already, or of something not pertinent to the discussion. As a result, the members are anxious to continue with the next item on the agenda.

Silent observers do not interfere verbally with the functioning of the group, but they seem to receive a lot of attention from the other members who sit there and wonder about the silence. What does it mean? It could mean many things. Maybe they are angry because people generally don't wish to extend themselves to someone with whom they are angry. One manner of not extending themselves is not to communicate with others. On the other hand, it could mean they are fearful. When a turtle feels threatened, he pulls his head inside the shell. Human beings act the same way. When they are afraid, they pull within themselves and shut themselves off from the fearful outside world. Silence could mean they are fearful of appearing foolish because they are unsure of the appropriate thing to say. It could mean they are fearful of the knowledge of certain members of the group or of the authority of the leader. Another explanation could be that they are fearful of being rejected if someone criticizes a suggestion, or that there is not sufficient trust in the group for the members to express conflicting ideas. Possibly it means they are uncertain what is expected and so confusion causes some members to be silent. Finally, the silence may indicate some are thinking, trying to assimilate what has already been said into their previous experiences and knowledge.[4]

In a classroom when students are silent, the teacher often calls on them to make sure they are paying attention. Sometimes, the leader does the same thing in the group, and consequently the silent members feel attacked or embarrassed because of their silence. A leader rather invites them to participate but leaves them free to remain silent. If the silent observers are consistently called upon for their opinion, they feel relieved of their responsibilitiy of intitiating interaction. Possibly, outside the group they are silent people too.[5]

Another kind of group member is the extremely dependent person who is willing to "rubber stamp" approval on anything the leader suggests. This kind isn't helpful to any committee because she/he looks to others to solve all the problems, to initiate new ideas and never challenge any suggestions. Such people may, look to the clergy person to determine how they think on a particular issue and then echo those sentiments.

As a result of the various kinds of people who make up a committee or group conflicts naturally arise. It's important how these conflicts are handled. One should not act as if differences don't exist and pass on to the next point on the agenda. Because of the tension resulting from the uresolved conflict, the members won't be able to devote their full attention to the next issue on the agenda. Another ineffective manner of dealing with a conflict is to allow the parties to engage in a "win/lose" battle. In this case the persons invloved get entrenched in their positions, become defensive and thus there is little change of communication taking place. Ideally, the leader facilitates the disagreement in such a way that there is a possibility for compromise so that no one is the loser. When a conflict occurs, a "win/lose" situation is more easily avoided when a specific idea is discussed instead of labeling the idea as a particular person's idea, e.g.,"John's idea." In this way a distinction is made between an individual and his idea, making it clearer the idea is being criticized, but not the person.

Group Phases

We often hear about encounter, sensitivity and growth groups which emphasize personal growth and getting in touch with feelings. The two kinds of groups which pastoral persons frequently participate in are not these, but are the task-oriented group and the team building group. The task oriented group is formed to achieve a specific practical goal and an example of such a group is the worship committee which prepares the Sunday liturgy. A chairperson is assigned to this committee who has the function of leading the members of the committee to attain unique themes for each liturgy and to choose appropriate music for those themes.

A team building group is formed to develop a more closely knit group and an effective working team. These people hope to get to know each other better and to feel free to relate to each other more openly and honestly. Such a group is often composed of the members of the pastoral staff or the parish council who meet for several hours or possibly for a couple of days at a camp in a state park to achieve those goals.[6]

Despite the difference in goals, various groups have some common elements. In the initial stage of any group there is some orientation, hesitant participation and a search for meaning. The members usually begin by introducing themselves to each other and give a little background information about themselves. The members usually hesitate to participate in the meeting because they are unsure of their goal, even though it has been clearly stated by the chairperson. People tend to wait and allow others to take the lead. They look to the leader for more guidance and help to begin the session. Possibly they begin speaking about the means to attain the goal and then someone asks for a clarification of the goal of their group. A common conflict arises at this point when some of the members seek to have their social needs met, and others become anxious to begin working on the goal.

In the second stage there is usually some conflict and often it is between the leader and the group members who come with different expectations of the leader of the group. Some members become disappointed in the leader because she/he is not the traditional authoritarian leader, who provides answers and solutions to questions and issues. Instead the leader urges the group to explore and use its own resources to attain the stated goal. Some members become angry at this. Since the leader is not leading authoritatively others in their impatience try to assume the leadership role in an attempt to "get something accomplished." This often causes some feelings of irritation among other members who object to the unassigned leaders becoming leaders. Friction toward the leader often occurs too when the members realize they are not the leader's favorite.

The third stage of development in the group is cohesiveness. Now that the conflicts are generally over, the group gradually develops into a cohesive unit. There is an increase in morale, mutual trust and self-disclosure. The members no longer are holding back their disagreements, but feel secure enough to voice them in the group without fear of being rejected for offering a divergent view. In this stage the members at times unite to such an extent that they organize themselves against the rest of the world to attain their goal. To do this, they suppress all expression of negative feelings toward one another.[7]

The final phase of group development is the group-centered, productive phase. In this stage the members are concerned about each other and about working together as a group, but not to the extent that they ignore or gloss over conflicts in order to achieve harmony. The members have learned to face conflict and to use it creatively. They have also developed a greater tolerance for differences in values and behaviors and have learned to use these effectively rather than allowing them to interfere with their work. In general, they have accepted responsibility to attain a goal and now work together to do that. It should be noted that the developmental stages of groups are rarely well demarcated and that there is considerable overlap between one stage and another, and that not all groups follow in this order.[8]

In the group interaction described at the beginning of the chapter some elements of the first two phases were present. There was some hesitation to begin the discussion and this stage was followed by conflict.

The different phases of groups were evident in two other groups in which I was present. I was asked to be a member of the energy committee of the hospital because of my concern for energy conservation. I went to the first meeting with high expectations of accomplishing a great deal and was frustrated when we did so little. We spent time socializing for the first several minutes. Then the chairperson called the meeting to order stating the task the committee was given by the administrative council and informing the group of the limitations of its power—it could make recommendations, but not set policies. Her introductory comments were followed by silence. As a group, we didn't know where to begin, we didn't know what aspect of the vast energy problem should receive our attention first. I remember leaving that room after 60 minutes feeling very disappointed and saying to myself: "This is going to take forever. We didn't accomplish much." The administrator of the hospital asked me later how things went in the meeting and when I shared my frustration, he said, "Well, that's what I usually expect from any first meeting. It takes time for the group to get to know each other before they can begin to work." This meeting illustrated the first phase of groups—hesitant participation and orientation.

In another group I was leading, I was reminded of all the phases of groups. This was a Professional Advisory Group who were giving me advice concerning my Clinical Pastoral Education Program. In the first meeting, after answering a number of questions and giving some explanations about pastoral education, I stated how they could help me achieve my goal and a discussion ensued. Then in the middle of the second meeting, one member surprised me by asking, "Father, is this what we are supposed to do in this group?" The person needed the goal of the group restated to make sure we were moving in the right direction. At this point, I realized we were still in the first phase, "getting oriented." After the second meeting two members privately asked how I thought the meetings were going. I commented they were going pretty well, but that I hoped to move a little faster in the future. Those members immediately agreed and said we were getting bogged down in details. Underneath their comments there seemed to be some irritation with me as a leader because I permitted the group to move so slowly. This illustrated the second phase of the group dynamics, some conflict. In the third and fourth meethings, I experienced the group as being a cohesive unit working on the stated goal of helping me improve the Clinical Pastoral Program and at the same time acknowledging differences. This group probably moved faster than others because the members generally knew each other for five years before becoming members of this committee.

Group Size

The larger any group is, the less members experience direct involvement and participation. Instead of interacting with one another, the persons often interact with the chairperson and this makes the leader very powerful. At the same time, the meeting tends to be merely an opportunity for the chairperson to give information to the others present, rather than an opportunity of engaging in real discussion. If there is to be a discussion, then the group must be small enough so each person has the opportunity to have the floor, to feel comfortable enough to express ideas and feelings, to interact meaningfully with the other members and to obtain feedback from them.

Since the Second Vatican Council, many committees and groups of various kinds have sprung up in parishes and dioceses. In the beginning since there was a tremendous effort to have every person adequately represented, the groups were usually very large. The priests' senate in one diocese had 42 members which caused a great deal of frustration and anger because there was no room for a discussion or spontaneity. In addition, it took too long to have something placed on the agenda and few results could be seen from the expenditure of so much time and energy. Then the bishop asked that the group be limited to 24 which was helpful, but the priests still found that the group was too large to achieve their goals. So they reduced it to 15 and now find the group more effective because there is ample opportunity for interaction with all the participants.

In a counseling group or an interpersonal-relations group (as is present in Clinical Pastoral Education Programs) generally fewer members are present than in task-oriented groups such as the priests' senate. This is necessary to allow for more interaction among the members. A few years ago in a large C.P.E. center, three supervisors led one large interpersonal group in which there were 15 students. In such a large group it was impossible for some members to receive adequate attention, it took more courage to request time and receive feedback from 17 other people, and it enabled some silent observers to remain just that, without ever being invited to share in the group. Some members benefited very little from that group experience. Many leaders of these interpersonal groups think that four to eight participants are ideal while twice that number is acceptable in parish councils or committees (task-oriented groups).[9]

Group Norms

The establishment of certain norms for a group is helpful so that group cohesion is attained. The participants need to know what is expected and what kind of behavior is acceptable in the group. These norms can be formal or informal, explicit or implicit. If the norms are to be effective, the members need to be aware of them and need to be willing to accept them. Obviously, members are likely to accept those standards which they understand and the ones in which they have had a part in selecting. For this reason it is wise for the leader to avoid imposing norms on the group autocratically without discussion.

Some norms that have proved helpful to some groups are the following three:

1. The members are expected to attend regularly and be present on time. When the members attend sessions only sporadically, the entire group suffers. Besides, members who attend regularly may resent the lack of commitment by those who frequently miss meetings.

2. The participants are expected to come to the meetings prepared to discuss the issues on the agenda and to do the appropriate reading and reflection before the meeting begins.

3. The members are urged to participate freely during the meetings, sharing their opinions and feelings as they arise. In this way the group will fully benefit from their experience and skill and the best possible decision is made.

Possibly another norm to be discussed is that of confidentiality. However, these are only examples and the important issue is that the norms be discussed and accepted by all the members. Many groups fail to achieve their goal because members are unsure what is expected of them and don't know what the norms are.[10]

Group Pairing

When pairing occurs in a group, this needs to be analyzed. Sometimes it is a method that persons employ to get into a group when they are fearful of becoming active by themselves. These kind of people chime in to agree with what another person has said and because of this participation, they feel part of the group. Later on, these persons feel comfortable enough to participate more fully and possibly have enough courage to disagree with someone or introduce a new idea. On the other hand, the pairing of two persons in constant disagreement usually means something entirely different. Sometimes it means they are expressing the sentiments of the whole group—all the members are angry, but prefer to sit on the sidelines and have their anger expressed indirectly through the angry pair. Other times, it means the rest of the members don't want to work toward their stated goal and so they encourage, or at least tolerate, the pair engaging in continued fruitless fighting.

If the members allow pairing to continue for an extended period of time, it could mean that they are looking upon the pair as an expression of hope that from their union the group will be saved and all the group's goals will be attained. After people struggle for some time to arrive at suitable solutions and only meet with failure, they eagerly look to two united members for hope that somehow through them success will be achieved.[11] Finally the pairing could mean that two members of a committee have had an extra group meeting and determined to work together toward a definite goal. This type of pairing is comparable to the "ramrod" method mentioned earlier. This puts the other members at an extreme disadvantage and has a disruptive effect on any group. If any grouping occurs outside the regular group, it is only fair that it is reported to all the members at the next meeting so that conspiracy is avoided.[12]

Dangers

In any group there are certain dangers. First, there is the danger of an attitude of *"don't rock the boat."* This causes the members to reach a decision without really discussing all the alternatives. Everyone secretly agrees to be nice and individuals feel social pressure to arrive at a quick solution. As a result, they do not voice any disagreement, permitting any decision to be approved. In this type of discussion the members short-circuit the group process in order to arrive at an easy decision.

A second danger to be aware of is the *"band-wagon"* effect. Sometimes, it happens that the first one or two speakers are very articulate and so convincingly express their ideas that they have a snow-ball effect on the group. Others support their ideas totally, and again there is no disagreement. Social pressure is also present to continue agreeing with each other rather than exploring all the possibilities. When this occurs, the leader might openly ask for any opposing views. It might be that there are none, but at least this kind of statement by the leader encourages other opinions to be expressed. In the sample interaction with the nurses in labor and delivery, this snow-balling effect seems to have occurred. Once the three vocal and upset nurses shared their opinions and feelings, it seemed that no one had the courage to disagree with them. In a similar meeting with the nurses on the afternoon shift, one nurse initially agreed with the idea of the inappropriateness of baptizing dead babies. However, when a number of nurses immediately disagreed with her and strongly supported the old custom of baptizing all fetuses and stillborn infants, she felt strongly outnumbered and feared to disagree with the rest of the nurses with whom she worked every day. She did not voice any opinion during the rest of the meeting.

Naturally, there is a danger of *one person dominating the discussion*, if the leader permits this. This means that one person is allowed to have more than his share of time during the meeting, with little time left for other persons to voice their ideas. This kind of person defeats the purpose of group discussion—seeking many viewpoints from different people. Group pressure needs to be brought about so others have a chance to participate. Sometimes the leader monopolizes the discussion and doesn't allow others to become involved in the decision-making process. This happened in one parish council where some laymen responded by resigning because they were angry that the supposed shared responsibility of the parish council was simply a farce.

A fourth danger is to allow the *discussion to develop into a heated argument* so that the parties involved spend all their efforts in winning their viewpoint rather than in making the best decision.

A fifth danger is to assume that *one person speaks for the whole group*: when a very vocal person expresses an opinion with emotionality, or when silence follows. Since no one is voicing a different idea, the leader is tempted to presume that one person has spoken for the whole group. This might be true, but it could be that others have different ideas and need a little encouragement to share them. It might be helpful in these circumstances for the leader to wonder aloud if anyone else has another idea on the topic.

In one group which I led, a participant loudly and dogmatically shared his ideas on how groups ought to be conducted, and at the same time angrily criticized my method of leading the group. Since his opinion was followd by silence, unfortunately I presumed the whole group felt this way and immediately began defending my manner of leading the group. My defensiveness only caused the entire situation to become hopeless. Later one member came to me privately and commented how helpful the group was for her.

A final danger lies in *hidden agendas* which hinder the group process and prevent the group from working on their expressed agenda. People come to groups for many reasons in addition to the expressed purpose of the meeting. Some come to meet their own needs as well as attain the goal of the group. This is a fact of life and is neither good nor bad, right or wrong. Problems arise when an individual's own needs inhibit the group from attaining its goal. These needs may be social or emotional, known or unknown, but they are there. So every group is working on two levels, the expressed goals of the group and the unspoken goals of the members. If these hidden agendas interfere with the group's functioning, the chairperson should assist the group to deal with the issues by bringing them to the surface and dealing with them openly. They need to be recognized and worked out. This does not mean they are necessarily dealt with immediately, but the members might openly decide to wait until later to deal with them.

A good example of hidden agendas occurred in a discussion group where it was clearly stated that the members were to read a chapter of the book each month before the meeting so that it could be discussed. All the members were given copies of the book well in advance so that they had ample time to read the first chapter. After the opening prayer of the first meeting, everyone looked at "Father" to lead the group even though one person was appointed the chairperson. When the priest did not initiate any discussion, the chairperson began to lead by giving some background material for the book and tried to get a discussion started by asking a couple of simple questions. However, the members responded to the questions with very brief answers or silence. The leader tried again to get some discussion started, but failed. During the periods of silence everyone looked at "Father" for some help and when he did not give any, the members felt betrayed. Why did he just sit there and leave them to struggle so much? Needless to say, the members began feeling very helpless and became angry at their pastor for not initiating some attempts to prevent the group from becoming a total failure. Finally, the chairperson turned to the priest and openly pleaded for help. Instead of answering their questions and helping to initiate any discussion, he asked simply what they expected of him. One by one they gradually admitted they expected him to do a great deal of teaching so that it was necessary for them only to skim over the chapter a few minutes before the group began. So their ''hidden agenda'' was that the priest would do most of the work. The chairperson thought for sure that the pastor would help him by asking better questions than he formulated so that the group would begin to function. The hidden agenda of the pastor was to be an observer and so he walked into the meeting determined to say very little during the meeting. Obviously, the hidden agendas of the different people had to be dealt with before anything could be accomplished.

An Example of a Church Group

I will present a role-playing situation to illustrate some points concerning groups.[13] The education commission appointed a committee to investigate an appropriate text to be used for the children in the Confraternity of Christian Doctrine Courses. For years the children in grade school have used the Baltimore Catechism, but now some feel there needs to be a change so that a more modern text is used which brings the benefits of modern psychology and catechetics, instead of emphasizing merely giving the children information. The members of the education committee are meeting on Monday evening at 7:30 in the basement of the rectory. They are seated in the following manner:

Mr. Robert Rules
(Chairperson)

Fr. Pete Sinens	Mrs. Constance Law
(Pastor)	(An interested mother)
Miss Beth Withit	Mrs. Virginia Octaviani
(Director of CCD Program)	(An interested mother)
Miss Mary Modern	Mrs. Dolorita Depress
(A new teacher)	(A veteran teacher)
Miss Victoria Fox	Mr. Ford Sheckles

(A veteran teacher)   (Finance Chairperson)
Miss Sally Smiles   Mr. George Truth
(Teenage Representative)   (Representative from Parish Council)
                    Mr. John Fidelity
              (A retired, dedicated church member)

The following takes place in the committee meeting. Mr. Robert
Rules opens the meeting by asking Fr. Pete Sinens to offer a prayer. Then
Mr. Robert Rules asks if all the members know one another, and when
they all nod, he states the purpose of the meeting—to decide on an
appropriate text for the grade school children in the CCD program. Mr.
George Truth requests more information about the various ages of the
children in the CCD program and wants to know the present text the
teachers have. The chairperson responds the children are from six to
fourteen years old and presently they are using the Baltimore Catechism.
Sally Smiles mentions she enjoyed her CCD classes because the teachers
were nice and brought the students candy sometimes. Constance Law
comments that last week's first Communion Mass for the CCD children
was simply beautiful. Virginia Octaviani agrees and remarks that all the
children seemed to enjoy their lessons. Ford Sheckles notes that all the
teachers deserve the gratitude of the parish because of their diligence in
preparing classes. Meanwhile Beth Withit shuffles her papers and Mary
Modern wonders if it is true that the CCD enrollment is down 10% this
year. Mr. Rules states that her figures are accurate and then urges the
group to deal openly with the task—do we think the Baltimore Catechism
ought to be discarded in favor of a modern text.

The second interaction begins with Miss Beth Withit giving an
emotional appeal to the group to change the religion texts and to use more
modern books which emphasize love and helping neighbor instead of
memorizing answers to questions the children aren't interested in. She
supports her proposal with quotes from Vatican II and from the pastor.
When she is finished, she nods to the pastor who becomes embarrassed
and says nothing. Silence prevails in the group until Mr. Rules asks if
there are any other opinions on the subject. Finally, Mrs. Virginia
Octaviani speaks at length expressing her concern for the children's

proper understanding of their religion and that they know the act of contrition for the first confession before their first Communion. Mrs. Constance Law supports Mrs. Octaviani pointing out the necessity for the children to know the commandments of God, the rules of their religion, the seven sacraments of the Church and concludes that she was taught with the Baltimore Catechism which didn't hurt her one bit. Miss Fox whispers to Sally Smiles, while Dolorita Depress, John Fidelity, and George Truth stare at Mr. Rules who looks helplessly at Fr. Pete Sinens.

After a moment of silence, Mary Modern initiates the third interaction by explaining how she feared God because of the education she received with the Baltimore Catechism and went on to say how the Charismatic Prayer Group helped her regard God as a loving Father instead of a Judge. As she concludes, she looks hopefully at Fr. Sinens who finally speaks noting that Vatican II urged the whole church to update itself and that part of the modernization process is to use a new catechism. He strengthens his arguments by saying that the National Catholic Directory indicates a change in catechisms is appropriate. His final comment is that something has to happen in CCD or else we will lose the youth of the parish. All the while he speaks, John Fidelity nods in agreement as does Mary Modern and Beth Withit.

Silence reigns in the group again as the fourth interaction begins until Mr. Rules wonders if anyone wants to make a motion since the discussion seems to be over. Mr. Law and Mrs. Octaviani pull their chairs away from the table, Sally Smiles chews harder on her gum, John Fidelity picks at his finger nails, Mrs. Depress wipes her eyes with her hankerchief, and Mr. Sheckles clears his throat nervously asking if it is proper for anyone to make a motion before there is some discussion on how much it would cost to replace the Baltimore Catechisms.

The fifth interaction begins when Mrs. Law and Mrs. Octaviani together complain how much damage the changes have done to the Church already. Miss Withit and Miss Modern interrupt, echoing their sentiments again, only louder this time. Fr. Sinens looks up at the ceiling while Miss Fox smiles cunningly as each person speaks and Mr. Fidelity continues his quiet efforts to listen to all the ideas expressed. Finally, Mr. Rules pounds the table with his gavel and requests that before persons speak they be recognized by the chair. After twenty more minutes of arguing, Mr. Truth makes a motion they investigate the problem more thoroughly so that a more agreeable solution can be achieved. The members readily agree that nothing can be settled at this time and the meeting comes to an end.

The readers might want to pause and draw their own conclusions about this group process before I comment about each interaction. Even though the chairperson clearly states the goal of the meeting at the beginning, the members are unsure what to do. They hesitate to really tackle the issue by gathering more facts and by talking about matters that are not relevant. Possibly they are hesitant too because they want to avoid a conflict which they know will result in discussing a religious text.

In the second interaction the group moves from phase one, hesitation, to some aspects of phase two where conflict occurs. The CCD director causes the conflict by forcefully stating her views and by quoting the pastor as supporting her ideas. This gave others the impression that there was a collusion between her and the pastor. As a result, the other members sat there somewhat helpless until they were rescued by the chairperson who asked if there were any divergent viewpoints. This helped the discussion because it gave the two mothers the courage to disagree. If he hadn't intervened in this way, the discussion might have ended there, with only one viewpoint being expressed. When the conflict occurred, some of the members became angry at the chairperson for not helping them return to a pleasant conversation.

Pairing has definitely developed within the group by the third interaction. This is evident by what is said and by the places the various members have chosen. The pastor, the CCD director and the new teacher have similar views and so they sit together to support each other. The same is true of the two mothers. Another aspect of the seating arrangement is that the persons with opposing viewpoints sit directly opposite each other as in a chess match. Although a chairperson is assigned, the members periodically look to the pastor for help when they need assistance. In the second interaction the chairperson hoped for assistance from the pastor, and now the teacher does after she has the courage to reveal some personal aspects of her life. So the pastor is viewed as a leader even though he is not the assigned leader.

The fourth interaction began with the group involved in a heated conflict, and nobody seemed to know how to handle it. The pastor has expressed his views strongly and supported them with quotes from important sounding sources, and so the others felt helpless to oppose their spiritual leader, but they clearly didn't agree. Their feelings were illustrated by pulling their chairs away from the others. Others displayed their anxiety by various nervous mannerisms. There was definitely an impasse.

Finally, the two mothers got enough courage to disagree with the pastor and together express some old pains they have experienced since the Church began changing. Since they are sharing with the group some old hurts that are still very present to them, they come to the group prepared to block any more changes. This is a hidden agenda they have as they come to the group. Unfortunately the meeting ends in chaos because several persons come to the meeting with hidden agendas like this, and there is little room for real dialogue and communication during the meeting.

Miss Fox continues throughout all the interactions playing her role of conniver. John Fidelity is the faithful church member who is the silent observer. Mr. Rules is the structurer and the expediter even though he ultimately fails, while Miss Withit, Miss Modern, Mrs. Law and Mrs. Octaviani periodically are the aggressors during the meeting.

Footnotes

1. Arthur X. Deegan, II, "Group-Process Techniques," *Pastoral Life*, February 1971, pp. 14-15.
2. Arthur X. Deegan, II, "The Priest and Group Decision Making," *Pastoral Life*, January 1971, pp. 18-21.
3. Irvin D. Yalom, *The Theory and Practice of Group Psychotherapy* (New York: Basic Books Inc., 1975), p. 477.
4. Carl Goldberg, *Encounter: Group Sensitivity Training Experience* (New York: Science House Inc., 1970), pp. 246-8.
5. Gerald Corey and Marianne Schneider Corey, *Groups: Process and Practice* (Monterey, CA: Brooks-Cole Publishing Co., 1977), pp. 41-42.
6. Carl Rogers, *On Encounter Groups* (New York: Harper and Row Publishers, 1970), p. 5.
7. Irvin D. Yalom, *Idem.*, pp. 303-312.
8. Merle M. Ohlsen, *Group Counseling* (New York: Holt, Rinehart and Winston Inc., 1970), p. 59.
9. Merle M. Ohlsen, *Idem.*, p. 58.
10. Gerald Corey and Marianne Schneider Corey, *Idem.*, p. 23.
11. W.R. Bion, *Experience in Groups* (New York: Ballantine Books), pp. 135-7.
12. Irvin D. Yalom, *Idem.*, p. 339.
13. Richard A. Donnenwirth, "An Experience in Groups," an unpublished paper, Bethesda Hospital, Cincinnati, Ohio.

CHAPTER NINE

RELATING ERIKSON'S STAGES TO THEOLOGY AND MINISTRY

In my own life, I have recently noticed certain themes recurring. Four years ago, I changed positions as chaplain, moving from a 330 bed hospital to a 750 bed hospital. Reflecting on that experience, I remember that initially in my anxiety in a new setting, I had trouble "giving" to the patients and the personnel because I wanted "to get" something before giving. After I experienced receiving some support from the personnel, I was able to give to them. Further, I observed that after the sick received love and acceptance from me, they were able to give themselves in trust to my care. So I noticed the theme of "getting and giving in return." (I wish to credit Rev. Richard A. Donnenwirth of Bethesda Hospital in Cincinnati, Ohio for the seminal thoughts present in this chapter.)

During my four years at my present position, I have made a number of changes in the Pastoral Care Department, expanding it and seeking more professionalism among the members. I have incorporated in the department most of my original goals, and now realize I accept suggestions concerning changes in the department with reluctance because my tendency is to be very cautious to maintain what I have brought into existence. This represents another theme occurring in my life, "to make be and to take care of."

In preparation for certification as a hospital chaplain supervisor in the Association of Clinical Pastoral Education, I studied Dr. Erik Erikson. After his study of Sigmund Freud and his work with many men and women as a psychiatrist, he concluded that human beings pass through eight stages from birth to death. Erikson notes in his book, *Childhood and*

Society[1] that themes from all these stages periodically recur in our lives. His ideas were of particular interest to me because they helped me attain a better understanding of life in general and in particular, gain insights about my own recent experiences. The themes from his stages made sense, too, as I studied my interactions with patients who enacted these themes under the stress of illness. My experience indicates that in all our lives there are major themes which recur. This is true in my life as a pastoral care person, as well as in the life of the sick. In ministering, I discovered the importance of noting the themes that appear in the life of the sick person as well as being aware of the major theme occurring in my life. In this way, I make use of myself in helping others.

It is my hope that the following ideas will bring greater understanding to lay, religious and ordained ministers of themselves as persons and of the people to whom they minister. I explain Dr. Erikson's eight stages, describing each one of them with its mode of behavior and its developmental task. Next, I integrate this stage of theme of life with theology, often receiving assistance to do this from the book, *Growing Up To God.*[2] Finally, I apply this to sick persons who exhibit some of these themes during their illness.

First Stage

In the first stage the behavioral mode is "to get and to give in return." In this stage, which exists from the period of life until the child is one year old, the infant is frequently seeking to satisfy his needs. He wants to be loved, to be fed, to be changed, etc. He learns to give something in return too, e.g., a smile. If the infant successfully works through his behavior, learning to get and to give, then he begins to trust people. For example, when mommy and daddy leave the home to go to a movie, the infant trusts they will return and not abandon him. In addition to learning to trust his parents and other significant people in his life, the infant struggles to trust himself because as an infant he doesn't earn love or care from his parents. So the developmental task in this period of the infant's life is basic "trust versus mistrust."

From a theological perspective, I refer to this period as "unmerited grace" because God loves the infant, loves us first while we are unworthy of his love, and we respond to that love by loving Him in return. We demonstrate our love by worshipping God. *Continuing on the theological plane, the issue of trust versus mistrust is reflected in our attitude toward God.* Do we trust God as a loving Father or do we fear Him and become anxious at the thought of being in his presence? The Bible extols fear of God, but when it does, it refers to fear in the sense of respect and reverence rather than anxiety which creates distance between ourselves and our God.

When people become sick, they come to the hospital "to get well" and give themselves, in a sense, to the medical term to diagnose the cause of the illness and to cure it. For example, to be freed from headaches, a person gives up his regular schedule and undergoes the discomfort of many tests to determine its cause. Another patient is willing to give up his limb which is gangrenous in order to save his life, and another undergoes the removal of cancerous kidney to live several more years.

In this stage, there is also a generalized fear of the unfamiliar and the large hospital with its many tests and medical terms which are like a foreign language to most patients. This raises the issue of trust versus mistrust. It takes time for the patient to trust the chaplain. Often rapport must be established before the patient lets the chaplain enter his innner world. If the patient has experienced a lot of trust in life, the rapport and trust occurs easily. However, if the patient suffers from a lack of trust, there is likely to be little rapport established in the patient-chaplain relationship.

Second Stage

The second stage of life is "to hold on and to let go" and is comparable to Freud's anal stage—the holding on and letting go of waste matter. This period, which lasts from ages one to three, enables a child to learn what is his property, his body, and what belongs to others. In other words, an understanding of self and other gradually evolves. Normally, in an attempt to attain some autonomy, the child engages in rebellion. Connected with this struggle, the child realizes there is a lack of control, a lack of knowing what is his and what is somebody else's. When a child, for example, is caught taking his neighbor's new bike without asking permission, to see how much better it is than his own, he feels shame and doubt. So the developmental task at this point is "autonomy or self-control versus shame and doubt."

Theologically, *this stage is comparable to the account in the Garden of Eden where Adam and Eve failed to act on the distinction, what is their property and what is someone else's.* As a result of their failure, they felt shame concerning their nakedness which raised the issue of lack of control of disposing of their bodily waste matter. Connected with this account is the temptation of the devil who urged Adam and Eve to eat the fruit of the forbidden tree to become like God. This aspect illustrates the struggle to understand what is self and what is other. So it is also the stage of personhood where I struggle to limited extent to determine who I am and who the other person is.

Sick persons experience some difficulty continuing to value themselves because they are no longer completely in control. As a result, they begin to doubt their worth and feel shame. If a sick person is extremely insecure, control of his life probably is important to him and, as a result, he struggles with the tension of how much control to give the medical team. If the patient is a business executive, having a great deal of control over other people's jobs and lives, then that person often finds it difficult to be controlled by another, e.g. the nurse enforcing the doctor's order. Thus, control is a basic issue with sick persons too.

In particular, stroke victims, those suffering from spinal cord injuries and cardiac problems experience doubt and shame because of the limitations their sickness places upon them. Cardiac patients might have more problems than others because externally they seem so healthy. Pastoral persons, in ministering to these people, do not blame them for their illness, but rather accept them realizing that their illness, with its limitations, is a loss which causes the persons to grieve. Ministers support them in their grief and emphasize what the patients can still do, even though they are handicapped in some way. For example, with the patient who loses his fingers in an accident, it's beneficial to be with him in his pain of adjusting. Pastoral persons speak with him in his shame as he gradually lets go of the functions he can no longer perform and as he holds on to the functions he can still perform. Possibly, the ministers can help to develop other aspects of the sick person's personality that are underdeveloped.

Third Stage

From ages three to six, the child engages in playing house like daddy and mommy. This play acting develops his imagination and creativity as well as enabling him to attain sex role differentiation. During this time the child begins to learn how to deal with his aggressive and sexual feelings. Guilt results in the child when he overextends himself and this guilt functions as a restraining force in his behavior. Erikson describes the mode of behavior of this stage as "to make and to make like" while he depicts the developmental task as "initiative versus guilt."

As I reflect on this time of life theologically, sin and redemption quickly come to mind. Peter denied Our Lord three times and rightly felt guilty about his sin. Jesus came and offered him redemption when he asked him three times, "Do you love me?" This stage further is associated with conscience formation when a person learns what is right and wrong. As a result of transgressing the dictates of his conscience by allowing his sexual and aggressive drives to go unrestrained, sin enters our lives and the person needs redemption.

Viewing this stage from the sick room, I think of those patients whose imagination and creativity lead them to dream of themselves as a movie star or president of some big company and now realize, as they lay in a hospital bed with a lot of time to think, that they will never attain that dream. Other patients who fit into this category are those who allowed their aggressive or sexual drives full freedom so that they now feel very guilty about their past. Other sick persons such as heart patients who retire early because of their illness experience this feeling of guilt too because they are not working, not doing their part in sharing family responsibilities or because they view their sickness as causing a disruption in a normal family life.

Finally, some patients feel guilty because they think they are responsible for their illness. I know one lady who fell down her stairs at home after having surgery for a new hip sock and, as a result of the fall, destroyed the new sock and broke her leg too. She felt totally responsible "for that dumb act because I should have asked my son to help me." Pastoral persons urge the sick person to express her guilt and then accept her as she views herself. Often this acceptance helps to reduce her guilt feelings and enables her to accept herself as a sick person. At times, though, pastoral persons challenge the sick person concerning her feelings of guilt by asking questions about her responsibility for the sickness, her previous acts of responsibility for her family, etc.

Fourth Stage

Successfully passing through the first three stages of life, children acquire the strength to cope with the fourth where the behavioral mode is "to make things, and to make things together." Children make things manually and conceptually, and, at the same time, learn to cooperate with others, especially as they enter school. Beginning in kindergarten, they learn to make things with clay and to make greeting cards for their parents on Mother's and Father's Day. They also learn to jump rope, form a circle, and learn other games where cooperation with the other children is necessary. Feelings of inferiority enter into a child's life when he compares himself to others, realizing he can't do some things as well as other people can. Reluctantly, a child even admits to himself occasionally there are some things he simply can't do at all. Thus, the developmental task from ages six to twelve is "industry versus inadequacy and inferiority."

The theology of 'good works" is related to this period. We are a redeemed people because of Jesus' love for us, his death and resurrection in our behalf. He gave us faith as a free gift because of who we are, not because of what we have done. Our worth, then, comes from Jesus and our good works flow naturally from our living faith. As James says in his epistle, "Faith without works is dead," and so good works are part of our salvation.

Some sick persons emphasize this theme because they aren't doing their normal work and, consequently, feel inferior. These people have a self-image which is built on how much they produce. In other words, these persons have the motto that "worklessness equals worthlessness," and so they aren't content just "to be," but must always "be doing." Some management people especially have difficulty during illness because they have attained constant promotions because of their hard work. Ministers urge persons with this kind of personality to realize they equate work with worth and invite them to form new criteria for determining their worth and the value of other people, especially their family members.

Fifth Stage

When a child becomes a teenager, he participates in a rite which indicates his passage into adulthood, e.g., confirmation or bar mitzvah, if he is a memeber of a religious group. As a young adult, he attempts to discover his new identity. He tries out different roles to see which one fits comfortably in his own attempt to know who he is. He desires to become independent and to be his own person. He tends to get an over-idealized picture of himself and the world; then he tends to become an absolute realist, the opposite of that idealism. So he vacillates frequently during this period of his life and, in addition, fights to accept his limitations as part of his own uniqueness. Thus, the behavioral mode of the fifth stage, existing from ages 13 to 15, is "to be oneself and to share oneself with others," and its developmental task is "identity versus diffusion."

Teenagers begin to question the value system they have been taught by their parents and religious leaders and further question the basic truths of their religion. As a result, they raise questions like: What is man? What is man in relation to man? What is man in relation to his God? What obligations does man have to God as a result of his relationship? What obligations does man have to his fellow man? And more specifically, what is his relationship to his parents, brothers, sisters, country? Finally, do I have any obligations to these persons? Teenagers ask these questions in an effort to be themselves and to share themselves with others.

The theme of this stage is particularly present for persons who have suffered strokes, spinal cord injuries and mastectomies. If a young man has played on the high school football or baseball team and then suffers a spinal cord injury, he attempts to be himself again. When that fails, he tries to establish a new identity. When a woman suffers a mastectomy or stroke, possibly she finds it difficult to share herself sexually with her husband. Many other hospitalized persons struggle with this theme because now they view themselves as sick and so attempt to determine their identity as sick Christian persons and perhaps try to be the "good patient" who conceals all his real frustrations and anger about being sick. Another tension is experienced when patients are treated as things or diseases rather than as unique persons. Pastoral persons urge the personnel to relate to the patients as unique persons by example of word. Ministers bring this notion of uniqueness to the patient by their manner of interacting with the sick and the chaplain of a hospital emphasises this point during orientation for new personnel and in other programs for them.

Sixth Stage

The lives of teenagers from ages 16 to 19 are marked by forming intimate relationships with people of both sexes. At this time a person tests how close he can get to another without losing his own identity. Two boys become almost inseparable, doing everything and going everywhere together. Steady dating with deep sharing of self too becomes the common practice. They lose themselves in a relationship with another person, only to discover later that human beings need space as well as intimacy. Normally, persons can't stand 24 hours a day of intimacy and this is best borne out on vacation. Two of the best friends go on vacation and after ten days "of total togetherness," they realize they need distance from one another for a few hours. If a person refuses to enter into a close relationship with anyone, he becomes isolated. There is no sharing of himself with another or receiving of another in his life, and so he lives in his own world, cut off from others. Thus "to lose and to find oneself in another" are the behavioral modes while the develomental task is "intimacy and distance versus self-absorption and isolation."

As one person draws closer to another, he opens himself to being loved and accepted, and to being criticized, hurt and rejected. In this process of drawing close to someone, it is likely that the person's ideas and values will undergo change. Thus, a teenager often changes his relationship to his parents and alters some of his values too. Naturally, this is a cause of tension between them.

Jesus exemplifies in his life this behavior of losing and finding life in another. He lost his life for us, and yet found it in giving himself out of love for us. Further, his relationship to his apostles exemplifies this behavior. For he spent much of his time teaching them, losing himself in them, and, at the same time, found himself and his mission in this interaction with them. For example, one day after he spoke at length about his kingdom, the apostles were arguing among themselves as they were walking along, who would be the greatest in that kingdom. Jesus displayed his own uniqueness at this point, clearly explaining that the greatest in his kingdom is the one who is the servant of all the rest. He also displayed his need for intimacy by being with the apostles frequently, and yet he spent some nights alone praying to his Father, and some other time relaxing with his friends, Mary, Martha, and Lazarus.

Finally, this stage exemplifies closeness and distance from God.

Oftentimes, we wish that our prayer life would give us a feeling of being very intimate with God. However, in reality there are many times when we experience a certain coolness in prayer—there is no intimacy with God. Another aspect of this stage is the experience of Christian fellowship with our fellow parishioners. There is a certain oneness worshipping in the same church and a deeper unity can result when people serve on the same committee.

In ministering to those confined to their homes or the hospital, the issue of finding and losing oneself arises in a unique manner. Ministers visit and offer their services to the sick, and generally make a contribution to the sick person's welfare. It is equally important for the clergy to realize their contribution by losing themselves in leaving the sick room. Henry Nouwen states, "In this way the memory of our visit can become as important, if not more important, than the visit itself. I am deeply convinced that there is a ministry in which our leaving creates space for God's spirit and in which, by our absence, God can become present in a new way."[3]

When sick persons are hospitalized, pastoral persons are aware that sickness causes distance in relationships, that patients feel cut off from their families and friends. So the clergy facilitates contact between them. If a person is a patient in an intensive care unit or in the emergency room, then he is likely to feel this isolation more intensely. For these patients and their families, sometimes chaplains seek to be the "conveyor" of communication so that this sense of isolation is reduced and, at other times, attempt to become "new family members" by their concerned presence. Experience also reveals that often psychiatric patients have difficulty with intimacy and isolation.

Seventh Stage

"To make be and to take care of" are the behavioral modes of the next stage while "generativity versus stagnation" is the developmental task. During this time people pair off and marry and from this union comes a desire to generate and to take care of the children flowing from this union. There is also a desire to generate things, to promote values in future generations, and to create one's place in life by attaining status in a particular profession. Having accomplished this, people often feel a need to care for the thing created, the values promoted or to take responsibility is greatly reduced.

Creation and co-creation with God are related to this stage from a theological perspective. We are co-creators with God of other human beings through marriage and we further create ideas, professions, and movements through the inspiration of God and the assistance of other persons. We reflect on our obligation to take responsibility for what God has given us in his creation, e.g., the environment and clean air, and to care for what we ourselves have created.

This theme recalls those patients who have been rendered sterile from surgical procedures, e.g., hysterectomy, tubal ligation, and severe spinal injuries. These persons come to mind because they can no longer procreate children and pastoral persons assist them in struggling with the issue of generativity. It's important also to consider people who are becoming elderly and, as a result, are struggling with the realization their bodies are aging. Some senior citizens experience difficulty in generating new ideas and even in maintaining what they have fought so long to bring into existence. For a few, the struggle is simply to maintain their own life.

Pastoral persons urge the sick and elderly to continue to create and challenge them not to give up. One young man whose arms and legs are paralyzed has become a counselor in a rehabilitation unit of a hospital, where he helps other people adjust to the limitations their sickness or accident has forced on them. Senior citizens are often only limited by their vision of what is possible to them. One man went back to college after he retired because he always wanted to obtain a college degree. I know of other men who, upon retiring, learned to play golf and now are very proficient at it.

Eighth Stage

The final stage in Erikson's list is "to be through having been and to face not being." Here elderly persons look back, reflecting on their accomplishments and the people they have known, those they have loved, and those they have lost through death and moving. The elderly need to integrate their lives as they come to an end and need to blend all their life together so they can see their lives as menaingful. If they cannot discover any meaning, then the elderly become disgusted and despair. Thus, their developmental task is integrity versus despair and disgust.

Theologically, this stage is classified as eschatology, the last things which include death, heaven and hell. During this time the elderly re-examine death and the meaning it has for them, realizing that it is approaching. It's a time too for them to deepen their faith in heaven where Jesus has prepared a place for them since their birth. I associate this stage with Simeon who viewed his life as complete when he saw the Christ-child. There were no regrets, no hanging on, no despair, but rather life as well as death made sense for him. He was ready to make that journey into eternity. Simeon's religious beliefs helped him integrate life and death and such beliefs can help other people too find meaning in life, in suffering, in aging, in dying, and in eternity.

Pastorally in this stage, ministers help geriatric patients through their remembrances to integrate their lives. With the dying patients, pastoral persons assist them to prepare for not being. When they have put their life together, they find it easier to die because they feel a certain completion of their life on this earth and it's easier when, because of their faith, they look forward to a life after death with their God.

Pastoral persons, in ministering to the elderly and dying, evaluate whether they can face their condition, or if they need to lie to themselves and not face reality. Rather than forcing the person to face the truth, the pastoral persons seek out the reason they need to lie to themselves and then deal with that need. For example, a person might need to deny his dying condition because he hasn't made his peace with God or because there are no provisions for the care of his invalid-wife.

To achieve solidarity with the sick, it is essential to know from where they are coming and from where I am coming. To be compassionate with an individual, it is helpful to understand what struggles he is experiencing and what struggles I am undergoing. As a hospital chaplain, I have been assisted in doing this by attaining some understanding of Dr. Erik Erikson's eight stages. In pastoring the sick, I keep his stages or themes in the back of my mind and bring them to my attention when a patient shares some feelings or struggles related to them in order that I can minister more effectively. In this chapter I not only described his stages and their application to the sick, I added the theological dimension because it provides the cement that unites these stages with the care of the sick.

Footnotes

1. Erik Erikson, *Childhood and Society* (New York: W.W. Norton & Co., 1963).
2. John J. Gleason, Jr., *Growing Up To God* (New York: Abingdon Press, 1975).
3. Henry Nouwen, *The Living Reminder* (New York: Seabury Press, 1977), p. 44.

CHAPTER TEN

SPIRITUALITY

Spirituality firmly roots persons in their ministry. Without it pastoral persons could easily become humanitarians or social workers. A deep spiritual life also unites all their qualities so that their feelings of sexuality, anger, authority, joy, trust and love are integrated. Spirituality and emotionality are one within pastoral persons and do not function independently of one another.

A lot of emphasis has been placed on feelings, but feelings are not the person. Much emphasis too has been placed on sexuality, but sexuality is not the person. Rather, a human person is composed of the emotional, the intellectual, the sexual, the physical and the spiritual. All of these are you and I—elements comprising our personhood. If we are crippled in one of these aspects, then our spiritual potential is hampered. In particular, there is a strong connection between our self-concept, our image of God and our spiritual life. There is a connection too between our ability to express our feelings and our spiritual life.

Images of God and of Ourselves

To develop a spiritual life, it is necessary to know who we are, but as we struggle to discover who we are, we are confronted with the question—who God is for us. The image we have of ourselves and the image we have of God are intertwined. And often associated with both of these images is our attitude toward joy and pain as well as toward guilt and sin. If we view God as extremely demanding, then we probably perceive ourselves as great sinners, deserving of pain and punishment. If we look upon God as a person who wants total obedience, it is unlikely that we can really feel happy about enjoying life. If we have a poor image of ourselves, then pain and suffering are due to us as part of our lot in life. If we regard God as harsh and punitive, we tend to think very lowly of ourselves.[1] If we can only be valuable, lovable when we are perfect, it's difficult for us to see ourselves as being very lovable. If we are only valuable when we are working or producing, it's difficult for us to have fun without feeling guilty. On the other hand, if we view God as a person who loves us with our strengths as well as our weaknesses, we tend to value ourselves more highly, tend to enjoy life. If we have an image of God as a merciful Father who forgives our sins as he did the Prodigal Son, it enables us to relax and be acceptable without being perfect. If we look upon God, not as some mighty Being who created the world and then lives far away from his creatures, but as someone who is with us in our daily lives, then it's easy for us to feel supported and not alone in the struggles of everyday living.[2]

Biblical Images of God

God's love for us is specified in detail by John when he describes Jesus' discourse on the night before he died. There Jesus prays to his Father, ''That you love them as you loved me . . . so that your love for me may live in them'' (Jn 17:23 and 26). It seems incredible but this is Jesus' prayer for us, that God the Father love us as he loves Jesus. This is difficult for us human beings to fathom because we would like to express God's love in degrees. We view God as loving holy people 90% and good people 70%, mediocre people 40% and half-hearted people 20% and sinners 5%. This is the way we love others; our close friends receive more than those we don't get along with very well. It's not that way with God. God cannot possibly give 100% of his love to his Son and 70% to us. He would simply not be God if that were possible. God can only give 100% of his love to everyone. When we read some of the dialogues of St. Catherine of Siena with God, we get the impression that God is giving her his undivided attention; she perceives God totally 100% interested in everything she has to say. This is accurate because God gave his undivided attention to her just as he is willing to give it to us.[3]

In the Sacred Scriptures, God revealed his covenant wherein he pledges himself to be faithful to us forever despite our sinfulness and ingratitude. He said, ''If they violate my statutes and keep not my commands, I will punish their crime with a rod and their guilt with stripes. Yet my kindness I will not take from him, nor will I belie my faithfulness. I will not violate my covenant; the promise of my lips I will not alter'' (Ps 89:32-35). This covenant urges us to look upon God as a faithful Father in all circumstances and evokes within us a response of adoration and humility, an awareness of God's presence in our lives. This leads us to an awareness of who we are, not what we have done or have not done. God's goodness calls forth in us an attitude of acceptance of our state of creatureliness. This experience of the all good God enables us not only to have a deeper awareness of the absolute fidelity of God, but also of his total acceptance of us as we are.

As we place ourselves in God's presence, we are before the One who is our Creator and our Father. We feel comfortable enough to place ourselves in his presence because we realize he has loved us before the world was created. We realize that we are not the result of fate or chance, but unique persons called into existence by the creative act of God's free love. We exist because God wants us, because God loved us enough to create us. The simple truth that God freely created us discloses to us that God is Love in his essence and also in our behalf. Thus, even before we approach him, God has accepted and loved us as we are. Since we ourselves have changes in our mood periodically, and at times vacillate in our love toward one another, we imagine God does the same thing. We tend to project our own changeability onto our Creator. However, he is constant in his love for us just as he is constantly creating the world in which we live. He is not spying on us, waiting to catch us in our sin that he might withdraw his love from us. On the contrary, he loves us totally without reservation and wishes nothing more than that we might freely choose to return this love.

The thought of our lovableness in the eyes of God is illustrated by the way that Jesus taught us to pray. The disciples frequently watched Jesus pray and were curious how he prayed, so they asked him, ''What do you say when you pray?'' Jesus responded that he prayed in this manner, ''Our Father . . .'' Jesus gave us the privilege of addressing God as Father. It is truly a privilege to address God as Father because Jesus, the Son of God, had this right and he desires us to regard God as Abba, Father or Daddy. This invitation of Jesus to address God on such familiar terms is not only another sign of God's love for us, but it reveals to us something about the Father's personality. It reveals his kindness, love, tenderness, mercy—his desire that we approach him on the same intimate and familiar terms as Jesus himself did.[4]

As we try to approach God, we often struggle to express acts of love to him, assuming the Father is interested in hearing them. As we attempt to express our love, it is important to realize that our love for God is not as significant as his love for us. Our love for God is secondary; God's love for us is primary: "Love, then, consists in this: not that we have loved God, but that he has loved us and has sent his Son as an offering for our sins" (1 Jn 4:10).

This love God has for us is the fulfillment of a dream because we all hope to have a friend who knows everything about us and still accepts us. We dream to meet a person with whom we can really share ourselves, a person who understands our weaknesses and loves us with these short-comings. God is such a person because he loves us with our hopes and disappointments, our joys and our sorrows, our successes and our fail-ures, our sacrifices and our selfishness.[5] It is easy for us intellectually to accept the fact that God loves us; after all that is what we have been told since grade school. Yet it is quite different to believe this on the "gut level." It takes a long time to believe I am accepted and loved by God as I am because, first, we don't accept ourselves as we are and so we find it difficult to love ourselves as we are. We know we don't always achieve the ideal, we make wrong choices, we fail to achieve our goals because our talents are limited. Most of us tend to be more demanding of ourselves than God, tend to have higher expectations than God, tend to be able to accept and love ourselves only if we are perfect. However, God accepts us where we are in our own individual lives, not as we should be. He loves us as we hope for healing in this area. Generally, this takes the experience of being accepted and loved by another human being.[6]

Secondly, we struggle to acknowledge God's acceptance and love because it demands the ability to trust. Spiritually, trust means standing on the roof of our home and hearing God say to us, "Jump and I'll catch you." The person who responds to that invitation has trust. In Erikson's eight stages of life, he lists as the first stage trust vs. mistrust. In our interpersonal relationships with other human beings, it is necessary for us to experience trust from others. It is necessary too for us to trust other people. Once we have trusted a human being, we can put our faith and trust in a God whom we do not see. Obviously, this refers to St. John's statement that we cannot love a God whom we do not see, if we cannot love our neighbor whom we do see.[7]

Therefore, the basis of our faith in God is our willingness to acknowledge our Creator's acceptance of us; it is allowing God to come into our lives. John said this in his epistle, "We have come to know and to believe in the love God has for us" (1 Jn 4:16). This is the content of all belief in God—God's love toward ourselves. If we examine the Apostle's Creed, we discover that it is nothing more than a statement of our belief in the love which God has for us. Twelve times in the Creed, we express in different ways the fact that God loves us.

Our Image of God

It is beneficial to understnad the ideal image of God. It is nice to know who God is for our pastor, our spiritual director, and the author of some spiritual book we value highly. However, the important issue really is who is God in our hearts. Oftentimes our concept of God is best illustrated when a person asks us very pointedly, "When you think of God, what do you think of?—judge, hell, critic, aloof, punitive, stern, warm, friend, kindly father, well-wisher, savior or Good Shepherd?" That one word or those few words give us a good insight into our concept of God because if God is a severe judge or a stern father for us, then it is not likely we want to get too close to him; it is not likely we want to form a close relationship with him because we fear him too much. On the other hand, if God is a loving savior or a merciful father, then we are eager to form a deep relationship. We are not afraid of him, but enjoy being in his presence.

One teacher assisted his students in gaining a deeper appreciation of their concept of God by showing one reel of three different films which portray God differently. First, he showed a reel of Cecil B. DeMille's *The Ten Commandments* where God is aloof, stern and punitive. God frightened the people with his mightiness, his thunder and lightning, and so they feared coming near him. They told Moses to bring God's messages to them. This was followed by a reel from *Going My Way* in which Bing Crosby played the part of the assistant pastor. Here God is not only extremely distant, but often doesn't seem too interested in us. He is too busy. Yet we can attract his attention if we do something perfect and these perfect acts win for us God's smiling approval. So our acceptance often seems based on our works. Finally, the students saw part of *Oh God* where the director depicts God as readily available, constantly interacting with us, and supporting us, but not to the extent that we become excessively dependent upon him. After the teacher showed the films, he asked his students to write the different concepts of God that were depicted and then to identify the one that most closely matched their own.[8]

Another approach in discovering God's identity for us is to examine two different concepts of God. One concept regards him as a person who loves those who perform well. This places a tremendous obligation on our part to live exactly all the demands of the Gospel. A second view of God is not to ground our security in our performance, but rather in the good news of God's love for us. Here we strive constantly to keep in mind his radical love for us no matter what we do and his demand that we love him, our neighbor and ourselves. This second view regards Jesus as an outpouring of the Father's love for us; Jesus is the Father's gift to us. Because we take God's love for us so seriously, there is an urgent, radical need to respond. Because we believe in the incredibly generous gift the Father has bestowed upon us, we have the radical demands of the Gospel.

While in the first concept we understand God's attitude toward us to vary according to our performance, in the second we simply hear the Father inviting us to love him in return for his love of us. We wonder how this can be so because our experience in life tells us that people are loved because of their performance. In our society we come to anticipate that others will treat us similar to how we treat them. However, this is exactly what the good news is all about—God's ways are not man's ways. God initiates his love for us and does not simply react to our performance. God so loves us that he sent his Son, who in turn so loved us, that he gave his life for us. As Jesus was about to leave us, he loved us so much that he gave us the Holy Spirit to stay with us, to give us strength and courage and to transform our hearts and lives that we might continue to do the work begun by Jesus.

Jesus knew his Father was a loving Father no matter what happened to him. He knew that his father would take care of him because he was his son. Jesus' security did not rest in performance, saying in effect, "All is well because I perform well." Rather, his security rested in the deep realization of his Father's love. At the same time, his security was not such that he thought he would never experience loneliness or fear. He had no contract with the Father that he would be protected from all harm. He had no assurance that he would only meet success and that people would always acclaim him, that he would never taste defeat, sorrow or pain, that he would never encounter indifference, enmity, betrayal, rejection or death. But rather, Jesus had the assurance that even in all of these, his Father's love was strong enough to support him. His security was born of love, not on how well he performed.[9]

Our Self Image

In attempting to know who we are, it's beneficial to reflect on our own personal history. This personal history includes our religious history which means that we grasp something of our early religious training in the first years of our lives, our grade school religious training and our teenage and adult religious education. Our personal history includes our relationship to our parents and the closeness or the distance we feel toward them. It includes our relationship to our brothers and sisters, our relationship to the children in our neighborhood and our relationship to our teachers and classmates. Things of this nature help us to understand who we are today because we have insight into where we are coming from.

Our behavior is indicative of who we are as persons too because it flows from our being, from our personhood. One individual isolated act doesn't tell us much, but a group of actions do. Patterns of behavior indicate who we are, what our priorities are, and what values we hold highly. If we constantly speak poorly of ourselves, criticizing our physical appearnace, our ability to relate to people and our poor intellectual capabilities, then this pattern indicates we have a poor self image. At the same time, if we are able to accept compliments from other people and are open to constructive criticism from others, this pattern indicates we have a good self image.

In examining who we are, some of us are tempted to view ourselves as composed of two separate entities, body and soul. If that is true, is the soul the only real valuable part of our personhood and the body something that is simply tolerated? Do we just view the body as an instrument God made available to us to ''save our souls?'' Then we probably only tolerate our sexuality and our feelings as well. In reality, body and soul are not separate entities—together they form the whole person which includes sexuality and feelings.[10]

In the screening interview to determine whether applicants are acceptable candidates for a basic quarter of Clinical Pastoral Education, a supervisor may ask them to name five of their strengths and then to indicate five weaknesses. Some have a good knowledge of themselves and a good self-image; as a result they can do this, given a sufficient time. Others have little knowledge of themselves and a poor self-image; as a result they can name only a couple of strengths and a couple of weaknesses. They couldn't bring themselves to indicate more weaknesses because they need to be perfect and cannot accept themselves as imperfect.

Since the Second Vatican Council, the Church has been more open to the findings of modern psychology and has provided workshops for priests and religious in this area. As a result, they find it easier to express their frustration at not being appreciated, not being valued by their bishop or religious superior. All of us need to feel wanted, loved and accepted, not so much for the work that we do as for being our own unique selves. One of the deepest needs of the human heart is a sense of appreciation and value for who we are. If we are only valued and appreciated for the work we do, then someone else might be able to do the work better and as a result, we would not be valued at all. When we fail to feel appreciated and valued, there is something broken in us. We are not whole.

A student who does not feel accepted by his teacher will not learn as easily. A nurse who doesn't feel accepted by the head nurse does not find the same job satisfaction. A patient who does not feel loved and wanted by his family normally does not recover as quickly after surgery as one who does. A person who lives without experiencing acceptance from significant others is living a life in which a basic human need is not being met.

Acceptance means that the people with whom we live give us a feeling of respect, give us a feeling of being wanted, give us a feeling of being worthwhile. These significant others are happy we are who we are and they celebrate our uniqueness. Yet, they don't gloss over our idiosyncrasies and shortcomings because that would be living an unreal life. These significant others love us with our limitations. The acceptance we receive from them enables us to be free to grow, free to trust, free to be ourselves. This love and acceptance from others gives us the encouragement to be the unique persons that we are. When we are allowed to display our uniqueness, we become an irreplaceable personality in our household or community. Probably to a lesser extent, the same is true in a work situation; when uniqueness is encouraged and when acceptance of each individual employee is present, then the employees flourish and experience a great degree of job satisfaction.

When we love and accept other people, this does not mean that we deny their defects, that we make excuses for them or explain them away. Neither does it mean that we agree with everything the others do or say. Acceptance means that just the opposite is true; when we deny the limitations of others, we are not accepting the whole person but only one aspect. We certainly have not accepted those persons in the depth of their personhood. Only when we accept the total person with all of their personality traits can we truly say that we accept those individuals.

Negatively, a lack of acceptance means that we don't give other persons the feeling they count or are wanted. We tend to take them for granted or ignore them. We tend to expect nothing from them and thus indicate our lack of value of them. A person who fails to experience self-acceptance indicates this by his irritating comments and actions which are clear symptoms of the fact that one of his basic human needs is not being met. Some of these signs are the following three:

1. Boasting: in a subtle or obvious way so that he receives the praise he wants so badly.
2. Rigidity: a lack of acceptance causes a lack of security in daily living and the lack of courage to risk one step to either side of the path.
3. Inferiority Complex: this simply defines the above conditions. The desire to assert himself, to impose himself on others, the excessive need for attention, the quick tendency to feel threatened, to exaggerate or to suspect others of talking about him. All of these indicate that the person has failed to experience love and acceptance in life.[11]

Just as there are signs of a lack of self acceptance, so there are clear signs of acceptance of ourselves. First, we acknowledge our own perceptions even though they may differ from those of other people. We respect these perceptions whether they are pleasant or unpleasant. Second, we are aware of our own thoughts and conclusions, our assumptions and judgments. We acknowledge the judgments about ourselves whether they are affirmative or not. We value our own judgments whether they agree with others or not. At the same time, we remain open to the possibility of changing our assumptions and judgments as we re-evaluate them in the light of new information. Third, we are in touch with our own and others' feelings and value both the painful and the pleasant ones. We permit an awareness of a full range of these feelings and do not feel a need to sort out unacceptable ones. Fourth, we turn into the immediate and long range goals. We are aware of our intentions and permit an awareness even of unacceptable conditions because they are ours. With difficulty, we are aware of contradictory intentions and struggle to assign a priority among others. Fifth, we reflect on our actions, realizing that underneath them are thoughts, feelings and intentions. Finally, we hold certain values which we have freely chosen and correspondingly act on them.[12]

In the past we often spoke of celibacy as unconditional love of God and our neighbor, and we esteem celibacy because it offered us the opportunity of giving ourselves totally to worship God and to be of service to others in need. Today we might rethink this in the light of insights of modern psychology and think first of unconditional love of self as a prerequisite for having unconditional love of neighbor and God. If we accept ourselves completely, we are able to love ourselves. This acceptance of self means total acceptance and not just the "lovable" aspects of our personality, but our total personhood. In detail, it means that we are called upon to accept our intellectual, spiritual, emotional and sexual qualities; to accept our femininity, masculinity, homosexuality, genitality and to integrate all these into the unique persons that we are.

Jesus once asked his Apostles, "Who do people say that I am?" They replied, "some, John the Baptizer, others, Elijah, still others, one of the prophets." "And you," he went on to ask, "who do you say that I am?" (Mk 8:27-30). Who is Jesus of Nazareth? He is a man like other men, a person who enjoys teaching, a person who spends much time in prayer, a person who is concerned about the poor and the sick and displays his concern through compassion and sensitivity, a person who is hurt, a person who at times becomes angry and frustrated by the lack of faith of other people, a person who enjoyed relaxing with his friends, and finally Jesus is a person of faith. He had faith in his Father's love for his people and spent his life doing his Father's will as he mentioned on several occasions in the gospels. He told us about acceptance and love in his own life by being a person who loved Mary and Martha and Lazarus, who loved Peter, John, James and Judas too. He taught us by his example and in his words when he commanded us to love God with our whole heart and soul and to love our neighbor as ourselves. Indirectly, Jesus was telling us that integration is necessary. We need to integrate love and in order to deeply love anyone, we need to begin at the beginning by loving ourselves as Jesus loved himself, his God, his Father and his neighbor.[13]

This integration is not something that is a new insight for us because it is frequently mentioned in Sacred Scripture. In Leviticus (19:18), in Matthew (22:37) and in 1 John (ch. 4), it clearly states that these two go hand in hand. *Thomas Aquinas insisted that all knowledge begins with sense knowledge and he is the most prominent example of the Church's insistence that experience of God needs to be rooted in human experience.* Today, theologians are continuing to espouse that idea by insisting that love of neighbor, love of God and love of self are necessarily intertwined. Karl Rahner clearly supports this idea by stating that love of neighbor and love of God are one. Sometimes, in our Church's history, certain mystics have wished to exclude love of neighbor in their concept of spirituality with an over-emphasis on love of God, but such an exaggeration needs to be resisted.[14]

When we take a close look at the traditional forms of prayer, this point is illustrated clearly. Formerly, we listed three levels of prayer, discursive, affective and contemplative. Discursive prayer was reflective and involved the use of the imagination and the intellect. In discursive prayer we read a passage from Sacred Scripture like the Prodigal Son and picture the father hugging his son and welcoming him back. We tried prayerfully to reflect on that scene we imagined in our minds. In this form of prayer, the intellect was used to a large extent. In the affective prayer, the emotions were emphasized. Oftentimes, we Roman Catholics used ejaculations to express our affection for God. We pray, "Jesus, I love you; Jesus, I believe in you; Jesus, be with me; Jesus, I trust you; Jesus, forgive me." All of these very brief prayers are affections in the sense that they are expressing our feelings to our God. Now if we cannot be emotional in our interpersonal relations with other human beings, how is it possible for us to be emotional or to pray affectively. In other words, how can we say we love God who we have never seen if we cannot express love for our friend whom we do see. Thus, there is a clear connection between spirituality and emotionality. Friendship is not only important for our emotional life or for creating intimacy, but it is also important for our spiritual growth.

In forming a close friendship with another person, dependency is created. We are dependent upon the other person to listen to us, to support us, to accept us as we are, to confront us and to forgive us. These elements are all part of a close friendship with another human being. However, this dependency is not a one-way street, but rather both parties are dependent upon the other for all these elements. So in friendship there is mutual dependence or an interdependence.

This interdependence was illustrated among five single girls in their late thirties and early forties who are very close friends, frequently dining and going to movies together and vacationing with each other. One of the girls commented how pleasant it is to be able to go to the phone at night and call up a member of the group to alleviate her loneliness, since she lives in an apartment by herself. Another girl commented it is nice to have somebody to go out with on a Saturday night instead of just sitting at home. Finally, one girl summed up both, "Let's face it, we need one another." This girl indicated she had insight into friendship—the need of one another for support, for alleviating loneliness, for acceptance, for recreation, etc. Such a person who understands the need of a friend and can admit this dependency, has the capability of readily admitting dependence upon God. If we do not have a close friend upon whom we depend, then how can we experience dependence upon a God we have never seen. Certainly, it is much more difficult when a close friendship does not exist. Naturally, if we can say, "I need you" to a friend, we can take another step and say, "I love you." Once again, this shows the close connection between affectivity and spirituality.

Forgiveness, Self-Acceptance and Prayer

Today we tend to gloss over many sins and call them something else as we make excuses for them. This reached such heights that several years ago, Karl Menninger wrote a book entitled, *Whatever Became of Sin.* It is important for us to look at ourselves in our total personhood, and this means to look at our sinfulness as well as our virtuous deeds. All of us are sinners and in accepting ourselves, it is important that we accept that part of us too. When we deny our sinfulness, we are simply fooling ourselves. We are wearing masks in order to cover up our real selves, but as we strive for self acceptance, it is necessary that we look at every aspect of our personhood. It is beneficial to note that the word "person" which describes our uniqueness is derived from the Greek which originally meant "mask." Throughout many of our lives we often play many parts, we assume many roles according to circumstances of time, place and those other individuals present. As we wear these various masks, we are hiding from ourselves and making the answer to the question, "Who am I?" impossible to answer. These masks enable us to run away from ourselves, to forget who we were yesterday and to fool ourselves into thinking we really are ourselves today. This kind of living makes us disgusted with ourselves because we are so counterfeit and, as a result, we try to lose ourselves in many activities. In this way, we hope to escape our loneliness.

However, prayer can assist in changing this mode of living when it is blended with some human experience of forgiveness and acceptance. With this human experience we are assisted in viewing God as forgiving and accepting, and so are more comfortable in placing ourselves totally in his presence in prayer. As a result, our pretense, hypocrisy and acting ceases as our masks fall off. We see ourselves with our sinfulness, and yet we do not become mad or rush off and commit suicide. We see ourselves as forgiven, accepted and loved by our kindly Father, not as condemned or oppressed by him. Through the grace of his acceptance, we are assisted in achieving a better self-acceptance. As a result, our relationships outside of prayer are affected. Now we can more readily receive acceptance and compliments from others, more readily allow our real selves to emerge. Thus our experience of acceptance from God and our friends beneficially affects one another. Ultimately this leads us to realize that we are creatures of a loving Creator, and sons and daughters of a tender Father who has created us absolutely unique, utterly original, a human being never to be repeated. With this awareness comes the awareness of the uniqueness of others.[15]

Prayer in the Life of the Pastoral Person

Before the Second Vatican Council, the forms of ministry were generally limited to administrating sacraments, celebrating Masses, visiting the sick, comforting the dying and the bereaved, caring for sick persons in hospitals, caring for the aged in homes for the elderly, and teaching in parochial schools and C.C.D. programs. In addition, mainly ministry was performed by priests and sisters. However, the situation is drastically changed. We see ministry being performed by priests and sisters, and also by permanent deacons, lay pastoral ministers, catechists, and many other people who don't hold any special office in the Church, but nevertheless are the hands and legs of Christ for people who are in need. No matter what ministry a person is involved in, there needs to be a solid foundation for that ministry. That foundation is prayer. If prayer is not an essential element in a pastoral person's life, then an indispensable element is missing because without it, nothing in our lives has lasting value. Without it, work in the Lord's vineyard begins to lose its attraction and becomes boring and a burden. Prayer gives life to our work; it gives zest to our living, it gives meaning to our lives.

Many times it is falsely stated that our work is our prayer, or we haven't time to pray because there is so much work that needs to be done. Other times, we say we pray on the run with momentary acts of formal explicit prayer in the midst of many activities. However, Catholic tradition and contemporary experience of the '70's emphatically indicates that a regular prayer regime is necessary. Without explicit prayer of some length of time, we pastoral persons will not take up our cross and follow Jesus, dying and rising with him. Prayer enables us to distance ourselves from our occupations and allows us to hear the Word of God in a new way, to heal our weaknesses and to restore the power of the Spirit in our lives.[18]

When I think of the necessity of prayer, I think of a workshop on marriage which I attended several years ago. The marriage counselor suggested that all married couples spend at least one hour a week together without the children present. During this one hour, the husband and wife share with each other the events of the past week and the feelings that surround them. Time spent communicating and caring is necessary in order for a marriage to be healthy. If we agree that prayer is a relationship to God, there's only one way to foster growth and to deepen that relationship—time spent alone with Our Beloved. It is also true that it's valuable to share prayer with others and especially with those with whom we are working.

Prayer is faith and belief in God focused on a personal relationship with him. It is the disclosure of one's self to another personal dialogue, it is what friends do together. prayer relates us to the Father, and to Jesus Christ who is brother as well as Lord, and to the indwelling Spirit who is God living in us. Prayer is a lifelong commitment to know and love God the Father through Jesus Christ and share ourselves with him. In prayer, we must be attentive to Christ's presence as we are to our closest friends or spouse. One value of our attentiveness to Christ is that we have the opportunity to evaluate our apostolate to see if we are doing God's will or our own, if we are working for God's glory or our own.

If we examine the life of Christ, we see that prayer, communication with the Father, was a frequent element. As he was being baptized by John, he prayed and the Holy Spirit descended upon him while the Father said, "This is my beloved Son. My favor rests on him" (Mt 3:17). When Christ took Peter, James and John up the mountain, he prayed, and while in prayer, he was transfigured before them. In the Garden of Gethsemane with the same three apostles, Jesus knelt in prayer and begged the Father to allow the chalice of suffering and death to pass him by. Before he chose his twelve Apostles, he spent forty days in the desert. The Evangelists tell us that Jesus frequently prayed alone, spending the night in prayer. On other occasions, he prayed in the presence of his disciples. On one such occasion, the apostles were so attracted by his prayer life that they asked him to teach them how to pray. That's when Our Lord taught them the "Our Father."

The final words of the Book of Revelation, "Come, Lord Jesus" easily serve as the theme of all Christian prayer because in prayer, we attempt to give our undivided attention to the Lord. It is our hope that by conversing and listening, we will deepen our relationship to God through Jesus. This prayer sincerely expressed involves risks because we are not expressing a desire to learn more facts about God but to encounter him as a person on a deep level of intimacy. A student of history may study the life of Christ to learn all the facts about his life. The same student might learn all about his sermons to learn his ideas and values. A student of literature might study the entire New Testament to learn its literary style. However, when a person of faith cries out from the depths of his being, "Come, Lord, Jesus, Come," an individual is asking to know God on a personal level. To encounter another person on a deep level risks change. How many people after they enter a deep relationship with another person in marriage are not changed? Each partner affects the other for better or for worse. Our parents knew this when they warned us in our youth to be careful in selecting our playmates. They knew that friends could affect us, our values and our behavior. So in our prayer, when we are open to having God become part of our lives, we are risking something to ourselves, risking the possibility of changing and growing.[19]

Prayer can take many forms; it can be words, songs, silence, dance, or the Eucharistic liturgy. It can be done in a group, out in the woods, in the privacy of one's own room, or in the presence of the Blessed Sacrament. However, no matter where it takes place, one thing is sure. Without prayer, the dying and rising of Christ "becomes less operative and cedes to worldly wisdom, the Spirit is muted and one's ministry and personal life tend to be motivated by superficial and selfish considerations."[20]

Conclusion

Pastoral persons need to be spiritual persons who are comfortable with God and comfortable talking about him and sincerely striving to live by his principles. However, it is necessary for us first to be comfortable with ourselves, to feel good about who we are. Once we have accepted ourselves, it is easier for us to acknowledge the Lord's acceptance and love of us. Once we have accepted the forgiveness of others, it is possible for us to accept the Lord's forgiveness. Once we have experienced an in-depth relationship with another human being, it is conceivable that we can form an intimate relationship with God.

However, a good self-image and relationships with other persons are not sufficient, we also need to have a good image of God. Hopefully, we can accept Jesus' invitation to regard God as a loving Father who is readily accessible to us. Then we can enthusiastically share this image with others.

There is an old adage, "You can't give what you don't have." In the area of spirituality, this means that we pastoral persons can't assist others in relating to God unless we ourselves have a relationship with him. It means that only a person who has experienced the Lord's love can speak convincingly about that love.

Footnotes

1. Audrey E. Campbell-Wray, "Belonging to a Punitive God," *Belonging: Issues of Emotional Living in an Age of Stress for Clergy and Religious*, ed. E.J. Franasiak, (Whitinsville, MA: Affirmation Books, 1979), pp. 54-57.
2. Nicholas Lohkamp, "Can Education Change Moral Values," The John Neumann Institute, Waterford, August, 1979.
3. Peter G. van Breenen, S.J., *As Bread That is Broken* (Denville, N.J.: Dimension Books, Inc., 1974), p. 14.
4. Eric Doyle, O.F.M., "On Being Human: Reflections on the Anthropological Value of Prayer," *Review for Religious*, Nov., 1974, pp. 1288-90.
5. Peter G. van Breenen, S.J., *op. cit.*, p. 13.
6. Gerald R. Grosh, S.J., "Theological Presuppositions of Contemporary Ministry" *Spiritual Life*, Fall 1979, pp. 5-8.
7. Peter G. van Breenen, S.J., *op. cit.*, p. 15.
8. Timothy E. O'Connell, "Grace and Growth and Growth in Moral Life," The John Neumann Summer Institute, (Waterford, WI, July 26, 1979).
9. Val J. Peter, "Two Models of Christianity," *Review for Religious*, July, 1978, pp. 493-5.
10. Nicholas Lohkamp, *op. cit.*
11. Peter G. van Breenen, S.J., *op. cit.*, pp. 9-11.
12. Miller, Nunnally and Wachman, *Alive and Aware: Improving Communications in Relationships, Interpersonal Communications Programs, (Minneapolis. MI, 1975), pp. 227-232.*
13. *Walter Trobisch, Love Yourself* (Drowners Grove, IL: Inter-Varsity Press), pp. 9-19.
14. Philip S. Keane, S.S., "The Meaning and Functioning of Sexuality in the Lives of Celibates and Vrigins," *Review for Religious*, March, 1975, pp. 280-1.
15. Donald Goergen, "Affectivity and Spirituality" *Spiritual Counselor*, Chicago, Ill., Tape 4, (Chicago, IL: Thomas More Association, 1979).
16. Eric Doyle, O.F.M., *op. cit.*, pp. 1291-3.
17. Eric Doyle, O.F.M., *op. cit.*, p. 1285.
18. Ernest E. Larkin, O. Carm., and Gerard T. Broccollo, *Spiritual Renewal of American Priesthood*, (Washington, D.C.: United States Catholic Conference 1973), p. 46.
19. William R. Plat, "Risk Praying," *Emmanuel*, May, 1979, p. 241.
20. Ernes E. Larkin, O. Carm., and Gerard T. Broccollo, *op. cit.*, p. 48.